A
GARDENER'S
CRAFT
COMPANION

ROCKPORT

First published in the United States of America by

Rockport Publishers, Inc.
33 Commercial Street
Gloucester, Massachusetts 01930-5089
Telephone: (978) 282-9590
Fax: (978) 283-2742
www.rockpub.com

ISBN 1-56496-850-2
10 9 8 7 6 5 4 3 2 1
Cover and Book Design: Mary Ann Guillette
Photography: Bobbie Bush Photography
Project Manager: Candie Frankel
Proofreader: Kathleen Berlew
Pattern Artist: Roberta Franwirth

Printed in China

GARDENER'S
CRAFT
COMPANION

GLOUCESTER MASSACHUSETTS

ROCKPORT PUBLISHERS

simple modern projects to make with garden treasures

SANDRA SALAMONY & MARYELLEN DRISCOLL

contents

introduction

Don't be fooled by the title. Whether you tend a bounteous garden in the country, an urban patio of potted botanicals, or none of the above, every project in this book is designed to be made readily and easily by anyone. All you need is an appreciation for the greatness of a garden and its vibrant colors, varied shapes, and spurring aromas, plus an enthusiasm for translating nature's elements into gorgeous projects.

The pages of this book will lead the way. But don't expect the same old wreaths and dried flower arrangements found in nearly every garden craft book of the past. We've filled each chapter with fresh project ideas based on up-to-date crafting techniques, current materials, and today's sensibilities.

The first chapter covers the basics: how to harvest fresh flowers, herbs, and other botanicals and preserve them for crafting. You'll find instructions and tips for the timeless techniques of pressing and air-drying as well as for faster and often more effective modern-day approaches to preserving the color and form of garden-grown goods.

With the basics in tow, the creative process begins. The chapters that follow offer a diversity of projects that highlight the natural beauty of objects found in the garden. There are many useful and decorative gift items and accents for every room in the house. Each project includes a color photograph accompanied by step-by-step how-to instructions. "Branching Out" suggests clever ideas for variations on the project shown, and "Inside Dirt" offers tips on obtaining, preserving, and handling the botanicals recommended for the project. Additional project ideas follow in the gallery.

So, read on, and let your garden (or someone else's) grow into beautiful crafts that will last from season to season—and never require any weeding.

the basics

HARVESTING

For all of the projects in this book, the first and perhaps most important step is selecting and harvesting the botanicals. Always choose blossoms and plants in peak condition, as the drying process will only intensify any flaws. If you are buying from a florist, ask to be shown the freshest flowers available. If you are harvesting from your own garden, choose flowers and leaves that are fully open. An exception is roses, which you may wish to harvest with partially opened buds.

It's also important to make sure the flowers are dry. No matter how beautiful they may look in the morning dew or with droplets of water glistening on their petals after an unexpected shower, do not pick flowers and other botanicals when they are wet. Extra moisture can cause discoloring, mold, and rapid deterioration in quality. On bright days, late morning is often the best time for harvesting. The afternoon hours are also fine as long as it doesn't get too hot and the blossoms appear healthy and not wilted.

It's smart not to harvest more than you can dry or press on that same day. Whichever preservation method you choose, begin as soon after harvesting as possible, certainly no more than an hour or two. Immediately after harvesting is ideal. Always harvest more pieces for drying than you will need for your project. Some will dry better than others, or you may be inspired to craft more and will appreciate having the extras.

It's also a good idea to keep a record of your flowers or botanicals, including where and when you picked them. Such information might prove helpful if you want to go back another year to find more. You might also want to incorporate plant information into the craft itself; for instance, you might paste a dried flower on a note card and add its botanical name in calligraphic lettering. If a dried item has a particular memory attached to it, such as a walk in the woods with a friend, you might want to keep track of it so that you can use it to make a personal gift for your friend.

Whether you grow your own botanicals or visit your favorite florist or farm stand to collect them, be sure to consult "The Inside Dirt"—a special tip box accompanying each project in this book—for insights and shortcuts on harvesting and handling. For more in-depth information on growing and drying specific flowers, consult one of the many books currently available on this subject.

DRYING

There are several ways to go about drying flowers, herbs, and other plant materials for craft use. The method you choose may depend on the resources you have at hand or it may be dictated by the craft project itself. Always read the instructions and get a feel for the scope of a project before purchasing or collecting materials. Three popular methods for drying flowers and other botanicals, including how they work and under what circumstances they work best, are outlined here.

Air-Drying

Air-drying is exceptionally easy. It requires little attention and few, if any, special resources. A bonus is the decorative accent air-dried botanicals lend to the home. Air-drying can be accomplished in several ways, depending on the material being dried. No matter which method you use, several important guidelines apply:

- Dry plant material in a relatively dark part of the house, as sunlight will fade the color.

- Avoid areas that are moist. That rules out basements, kitchens, and bath-rooms. Suitable places can include attics, large closets, a garage, or a garden shed. If you live in a relatively humid climate or if you are drying during a wet or humid time of year, run a dehumidifier in the drying area.

- Choose a well-ventilated space. Air needs to be able to circulate around objects left to dry to preserve them effectively.

Hanging

Hanging flowers to dry takes nothing more than a twist-tie to clasp the flowers in bundles, plus string and a hook or nail from which to hang them. The drawback is that natural drying takes time, from one week up to a month or more, depending on the plant material. It is most effective with herbs and compact flowers, such as peony buds, rosebuds, safflower buds, delphiniums, chive flowers, and partially opened marigolds. It is not the optimum choice for flowers that readily shed their petals, such as black-eyed Susans or daisies. Flowers with delicate structures that could be compromised when bunched together should also not be dried in this fashion. Here are the basics:

- Assemble the flowers in small bundles, about eight to ten stems each. If the bundles are too bulky, the flowers or plant material in the interior may not properly dry.

- Bundle the same kind of flowers together. Choose flowers that are the same size and at the same stage of blossoming for each bundle, so that they dry at an even rate.

- Bind the bundled stems together at the cut end with a twist-tie. String also works, but a twist-tie is more readily tightened as the stems dehydrate and shrink.

- Tie string around each bundle and hang from a hook or nail.

- Examine the stems for an excess of leaves, and pull some or all of them off. Usually, there are more leaves on a stem than look attractive once dry. Also, a cluttering of leaves can impede the flow of air. If you're undecided on how much to trim off, use discretion. You can pull off more leaves after they are dry.

Screen

Screen-drying is ideal for flowers that splay out flat, such as cosmos, anemones, feverfew, and daisies, and for bulky flowers that might be compressed or disfigured if hung upside down. It is also the preferred way to dry individual petals.

The technique is simple: Prop an old window screen horizontally on a couple of sawhorses or crates. To dry whole flowers, insert the stem down through the mesh weave so that the flower rests on top of the screen. Don't place the flowers too closely together, and make sure none of the petals or leaves overlap. The air must be able to circulate freely on all sides for effective, even drying.

If the weave on a screen is too fine for running stems through, clip larger openings with wire cutters. You can also improvise with larger, more open wire meshes, such as chicken wire. If the blossom on a flower is too small or delicate to hang from a larger mesh, slip a large paper clip up the stem to straddle the mesh. For a small decorative screen, try holding cheesecloth taut in an embroidery hoop.

Naturally

Some flowers dry practically on their own. Everlastings, as the name implies, are particularly well suited to natural drying. All you need to do is set the flowers in a vase with about ½" (1 cm) of water to start. The water will be absorbed and evaporate in no time, and the flowers will continue to dry on their own. Other flowers well-suited to this no-nonsense approach include strawflowers, hydrangeas, globe amaranth, yarrow, heather, Chinese lanterns, baby's breath, statice, and honesty. Ornamental grasses also drape nicely when dried this way.

Using Desiccants

Another method for drying flowers is to cover them with a drying agent, or desiccant. The most popular desiccant in use today is silica gel, a sandlike substance available from garden stores, craft supply stores, and some florists under a variety of trade names. It is ideal for drying flowers because it works relatively quickly and effectively—the drying time can range from three to seven days—and it preserves the color and shape of the item being dried.

To use silica gel, you will need several airtight containers. Limit each container to one type of flower or plant material at a time, to avoid having different kinds of materials drying at different rates. Place ½" (1 cm) to 1" (3 cm) of silica gel in the bottom of the container to create a base. Trim off the stem, leaving 1" (3 cm) to 2" (5 cm), and then proceed as follows:

1 | Place flat-faced flowers, such as Gerber daisies, facedown into the silica gel.

2 | Lay bell-shaped or spiked flowers, such as snapdragons, horizontally on their sides.

3 | Place flowers with many layers of overlapping petals, such as dahlias, peonies, and marigolds, faceup on the gel. Carefully sprinkle granules in between the overlapping petals, using tweezers to gently lift and separate the layers, if necessary.

Make sure none of the flowers that are placed on the gel touch or overlap one another. Then gently sift more silica gel over and around the flowers until they are fully covered. Work slowly, so that the petals remain in their natural position and are not crushed. Add more layers of flowers and silica gel if space permits.

Close the container, and add a label with the date and flower name. Store the container in a relatively dark, dry area of the house, but in view, so that you will remember to check it periodically. Begin checking on the second day of drying. Delicate flowers with thin petals may dry in just under three days. Bulkier flowers could take as long as one week.

4 | When the flowers or plant materials are crisp and feel dry, carefully remove the silica gel, and pull out the dried items with tweezers. Any dusty residue can be removed with a soft, dry artist's brush. To reuse the silica gel, simply dehydrate it in the oven, following the manufacturer's instructions.

PRESSING

Many projects in this book require flowers in two-dimensional form—that is, they need to be pressed. Botanicals particularly well suited to pressing include ferns, leaves, and flowers with thin petals and little layering—pansies, clematis, violas, lobelia, delphiniums, and petunias, for example. Flowers with many layers of petals, such as zinnias and peonies, can be pressed by disassembling the flower into individual petals. Once the petals are pressed dry, they can be reassembled to mimic the form of the flower or used separately as accents.

Like the other drying methods, pressing is easy to do. If you're just learning to press flowers or plan to press only a small amount, you can easily do so with books. Set the items to be pressed between two sheets of blotting paper, or other absorbent paper, and place the sandwiched layers between the pages of a large, heavy book, such as a telephone directory. You will only be able to insert a few pages of pressed flowers in a book before it gets bulky and presses ineffectively. Weigh down the book with additional books or some other flat, heavy object, such as a cast-iron pan.

A flower press has decided advantages over the book method. If you do your harvesting on hikes in the woods, you can take a small press along with you and begin the pressing process immediately. Another advantage to using a press is that it is orderly. When you press flowers and botanicals between the pages of various books, it's easy to lose track of them.

Professional flower presses come with blotting paper and cardboard sheets. To use a press, place the flowers and plant matter between the sheets of blotting paper. Stack these "sandwiches," interleaved with the cardboard sheets, on the press bed. Put the top back on the press and tighten until the layers are held secure. Wait at least a week before checking the progress of your pressed items. If the plant or flower is not yet completely dry, put it back in the press for another five to seven days. Once the flower is dry, lift it with tweezers. If it sticks, use the tip of a paring knife or craft knife to gently lift it.

For better flower drying:

• Place flowers and other plant material facedown on the blotting paper.

• Choose items of equal thickness to press together.

• Do not allow plant materials to touch each other.

• If the base of a flower is bulky, use small scissors to trim off as much
  as possible on the stem side without causing any of the petals to fall off.

• If the flower is delicate but has a thick stem, avoid air pockets by either
  cutting off the stem to dry separately or slicing down the stem with a craft
  knife to create a flatter surface.

• Let the stems bow or curve as they are inclined. Straight lines can look
  stiff and unnatural.

STORING AND PRESERVING

All dried botanicals should be stored between layers of tissue paper in sealed containers or cardboard boxes. It cannot hurt to include a sprinkling of silica gel on the bottom of the box or container to absorb any lingering moisture or humidity. Pressed flowers may be stored between sheets of tissue paper in a large, manila envelope, along with a cardboard insert to prevent bending. Always label and date your packages, and store them away from sunlight, insects, and sources of moisture.

Use similar logic with any projects you craft from your dried flowers, leaves, or other plant material. Display finished projects in a relatively dry part of the house unless, of course, the dried item has been protected with a sealer coat, such as in decoupage.

To help preserve dried flowers, you can apply a light coat of hair spray or clear lacquer spray, available in craft stores. If a flower seems delicate and likely to fall apart, put a drop of clear-drying glue at the blossom center and on the back of flower base, where the petals connect to the stem.

Pressed flowers tend to fade, even when properly stored. They can be brightened with watercolors. Simply place the flower on a paper towel and lightly touch up with water-thinned paint, brushing from the center outward.

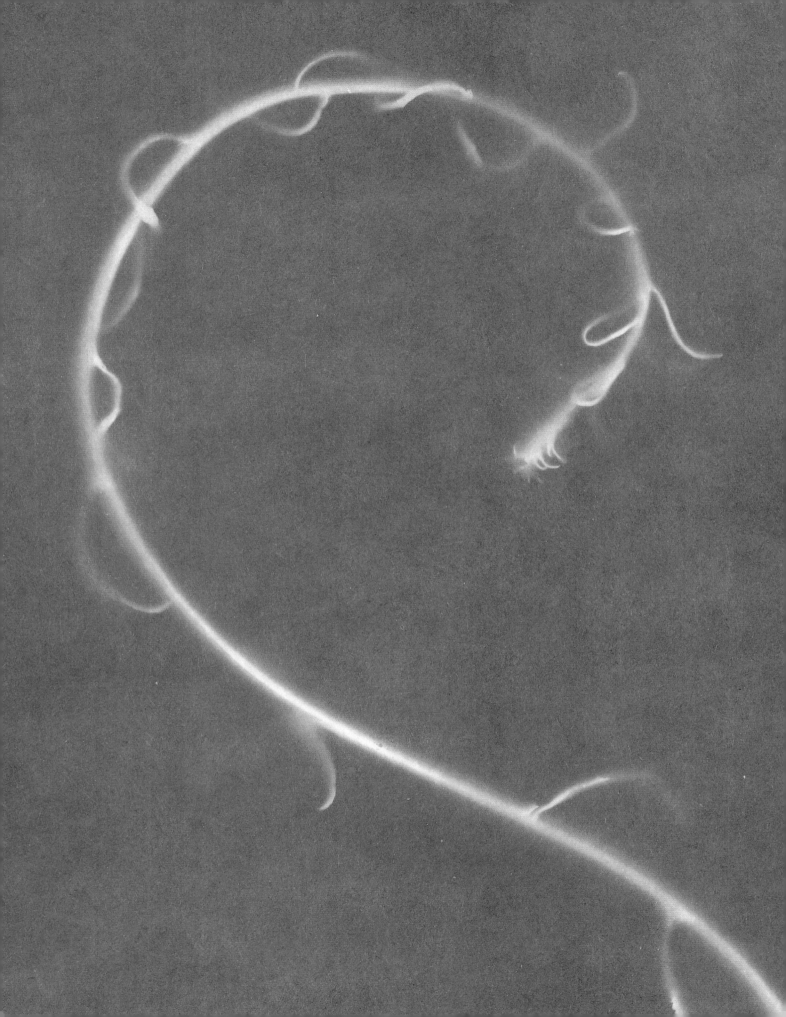

This chapter is all about capturing brilliant seasonal colors in bloom before they fade into a state of winter rest. Cluster romantically rich red roses (from the garden or from an admirer) into the suiting shape of a heart set in a shadow box. Dot everyday terra-cotta flowerpots with the cheerful faces of pansies, plentiful in both spring and fall. Or, wrap your favorite, most vibrant botanicals around handmade clay napkin rings to brighten the dinner table long after a fresh bouquet would have wilted.

colors in bloom

This is just a sampling of the everyday objects that can be enhanced with colors at peak bloom. Many of the projects in this chapter use flowers that air-dry particularly well. Sunlight will quickly fade color brilliance, so if you do air-dry your selections, be sure to choose a dark, dry location with ample air circulation. For more details on pressing and drying, refer to The Basics, beginning on page 9.

rose heart shadow boxes

Garden roses provide the vivid colors in these folk art—inspired shadow boxes. If you are cutting your own roses for this project, wait until the morning dew has dried. If you are purchasing roses from a florist, look for youthful, well-formed heads with no signs of mold.

MATERIALS

dried roses in two or three shades*

unfinished wood shadow boxes*

dry floral foam

dark mahogany wood stain

craft acrylic paint in cream and green

clear furniture paste wax

dark bronze dry artist's pigment

low-temperature glue gun

glue sticks

hair dryer

sharp knife

scissors

foam brushes

fine sandpaper

clean, soft cloths

*Approximately 36 red garden roses and 30 yellow spray roses fill the 6" x 6" (15 cm x 15 cm) shadow box at the far right

1. Paint each shadow box, applying dark mahogany stain as a base coat followed by two coats of cream or green acrylic paint; let dry after each coat. Sand off some of the paint along the edges to reveal the underlying stain. To further age the boxes, mix a small amount of clear furniture paste wax with a pinch or two of dark bronze dry artist's pigment. Wipe the tinted wax on the frame with a soft cloth, and let it stand for a few minutes. Wipe off the excess wax and polish the frame with a clean soft cloth.

2. Use a sharp knife to cut the floral foam into slices ½" (1 cm)-thick. Arrange the foam pieces in a single layer on the floor of each shadow box, trimming it to fit. Glue the pieces in place using a low-temperature glue gun.

3. Carefully trim the stems from the roses, leaving just enough so that the top of the flower head will be flush with the edge of the shadow box when the stem is inserted in the foam. Stand the roses upright in the foam to create a large heart outline, and glue in place. Use smaller roses to define the points and curves as needed.

4. When the heart outline is complete, fill in the interior, placing the roses as close together as possible. Use roses of a different color to create a smaller heart within, if desired (see the shadow box at the left in the photo). If a rose is too large for a given space, strip off the outer petals one by one until it fits.

5. Glue on roses of a different color to fill in the background around the heart, right up to the frame edges. Once again, strip away the outer petals as needed for a snug fit.

6. Melt any "spiderwebs" of dried glue by aiming a hair dryer briefly over the entire shadow box.

BRANCHING OUT

Vary the dried flower selection to create new color and texture combinations. For example, use dried daisies, strawflowers, globe amaranth, or asters. Create other vivid graphic designs, such as Mondrian-inspired color blocks, circles, and stars, or even mimic a giant flower shape.

THE INSIDE DIRT

• Air-drying compromises the color of roses. Fresh red roses darken, yellow roses fade, and white roses discolor. To most effectively preserve the color, dry roses in silica gel.

• Test for dryness by gently squeezing the rosebud. If it feels soft in the center, allow more time to dry.

• Lightly apply hair spray or a hardening spray to discourage dried buds from crumbling.

BRANCHING OUT

Many objects lend themselves to crafting with whole pressed flowers. Try decorating picture frames, jewelry boxes, and lamp shades. Experiment with anemones, dogwood, primroses, hibiscus, bidens, and daisies. Hydrangea leaves, ferns, and Japanese maple leaves also create a pleasing effect.

THE INSIDE DIRT

• When petals overlap considerably, gently pluck the underlayer petals and press them separately. Then "rebuild" the flower by gluing the petals to the project one by one.

• Varnish will cause some colors to fade, so test it on a variety of pansies beforehand.

pressed pansy pots

Giant pansies put their best faces forward on these colorful painted pots. Choose a color palette that will both complement both your decor and show off the pansies.

MATERIALS

pressed giant pansies

terra-cotta pots

craft acrylic paint in blue, lavender, green, and white

white craft glue

satin water-based varnish

soft paintbrush

foam brushes

tweezers

clean, soft cloths

1. Using a foam brush, apply a coat of satin water-based varnish to each pot, inside and out, as a sealer. Let dry.

2. Paint each pot with two solid coats of blue, lavender, or green acrylic paint, letting dry completely after each coat.

3. Mix one part white acrylic paint with one part water. Use a clean, soft cloth to apply this whitewash to each pot. Wipe around the pot in one direction, then use a slightly damp, clean section of the cloth to remove the excess whitewash where desired. Leave the rim of the pot in the solid color for contrast. Let dry.

4. Use a soft paintbrush to apply white craft glue to the back of a giant pansy. Lift the pansy with tweezers and carefully place it on the pot surface. Press lightly with your fingertips to seal the petal edges. If the petals on your dried pansies have separated, glue them on one by one. Let dry.

5. Apply four to six coats of satin water-based varnish to the outside of each pot, letting dry completely after each coat.

sewn seed-packet greeting cards

Give the gift of a garden by sending a greeting card complete with seeds. Use pressed flowers or petals from the same plant to provide a visual reference.

MATERIALS

pressed flowers and their corresponding seeds*

watercolor paper

purchased envelopes

sheer white organza

thread in desired color

sewing machine

scissors

*Marigolds and giant pansies are shown

1 | Trim a sheet of watercolor paper and fold it with the grain to make a card that fits the purchased envelope.

2 | Cut a rectangle of sheer organza at least 1" (3 cm) wider than the pressed flower, and twice as long as it is wide. Pull a few threads all around to fringe the edges.

3 | Unfold the card, lay it flat, and center the organza rectangle on the front cover. Set the sewing machine to a long stitch length. Using matching or contrasting thread, machine-stitch along the bottom and two side edges of the organza, criss-crossing the stitching lines at the lower corners. Trim the threads.

4 | Carefully fill the bottom half of the organza pocket with pressed flowers or petals. You may need to lightly shake the card or use a toothpick to force the flowers to the bottom. Stitch across the organza at the middle to seal the flowers in the fabric pocket. Fill the top half of the pocket with seeds, and stitch across the top of the organza to finish.

5 | If desired, write the name of the flower across the bottom of the card, along with the date for season identification.

BRANCHING OUT

Create a see-through window by cutting a
rectangle in the card front slightly smaller
than the organza rectangle. Sew two pieces
of organza to the card front, enclosing the
pressed flower and seeds between them.
Or, use this seed packet technique on
scrapbook pages to make a heritage
garden journal to hold seeds for the next
growing season.

THE INSIDE DIRT

Generally, seeds should be stored in a cool,
dry, dark location. To protect against moisture, place the seeds in paper envelopes
and then place the envelopes inside plastic
zipper-locked bags along with a sprinkling
of silica gel. When stored properly, seeds
potentially can keep for several years.

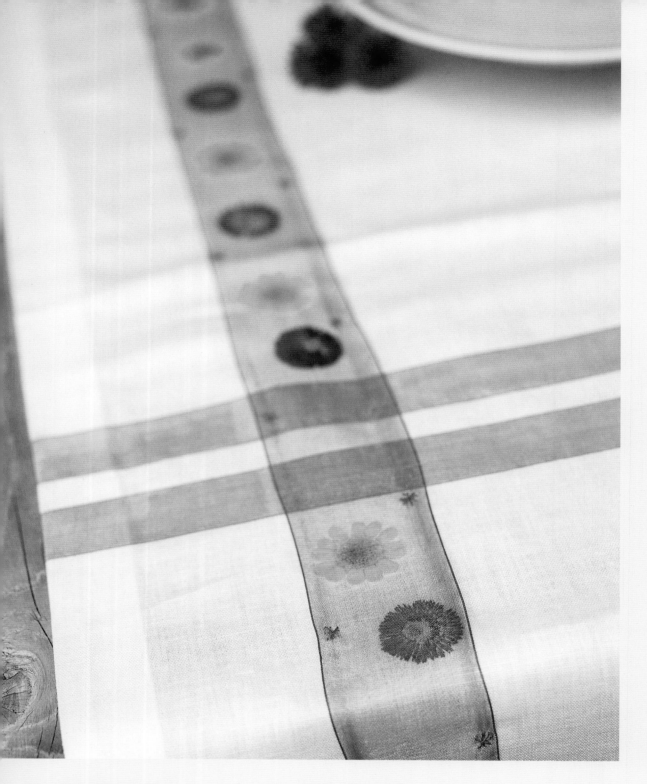

BRANCHING OUT

Modify the length and width of this runner to design place mats, a square cloth lining for a basket, or an extra-long runner to drape across a bed. On larger pieces, try using several wide ribbons for the flower inserts. Play with different-sized ribbons and flowers.

THE INSIDE DIRT

To coordinate the colors for this project, choose and press your flowers first. Then bring a sampling of the flowers with you to the fabric store to pick out the ribbon and fabric.

table runner with pressed flowers

Pressed flowers peek through a sheer ribbon on this easy-to-assemble table runner. No sewing machine is needed—the ribbons are bound in place with fusing tape and tiny, hand-embroidered stars. The pressed flowers are removable, which means you can display different selections from season to season or from year to year.

MATERIALS

assorted pressed flowers*	iron
2 yards (1.8 m) linen fabric	hand-sewing needle
2 yards (1.8 m) 2"-wide (5 cm) sheer ribbon	pins
2 yards (1.8 m) 1"-wide (3 cm) sheer ribbon	ruler
cotton sewing thread to match ribbon	scissors
narrow paper-backed fusing tape	*English daisies are shown

1. Gently wash and dry the linen fabric, and iron smooth. Cut a 72" x 17" (183 cm x 43 cm) rectangle from the fabric.

2. Fold and press the longer edges ½" (1 cm) and then 1" (3 cm) to the wrong side for a clean edge. Fuse the folded hem in place with fusing tape, following the manufacturer's instructions. For easier handling, cut the tape into short lengths for fusing.

3. Place the 2"-wide (5 cm) ribbon along the length of the runner, offsetting it 3" (8 cm) from one long edge, or as desired. Pin in place. Thread the needle with a double strand of thread. To tack the ribbon to the runner, embroider three over-lapping straight stitches in a star shape every 4" (10 cm) along both ribbon edges. Offset the stars from edge to edge so that they do not fall directly opposite each other. Tie off each design separately; do not carry the thread across the back of the runner.

4. Repeat step 2 to hem the short edges of the runner. Fold the hemmed section diagonally at the corners, for a mock miter, and hand-sew in place.

5. Cut the 1"-wide (3 cm) ribbon into four equal lengths. Place these ribbons, in pairs, across the width of the runner, about 8" (20 cm) in from each end and about ½" (1 cm) apart. Fuse down each edge, except where the ribbons cross the wider ribbon. Fold and fuse the ends to the wrong side of the runner.

6. Insert pressed flowers under the wider ribbon, interspersing them as desired.

flower tile mosaic jewelry box

Flower tiles are made by sandwiching desiccant-dried primroses between small glass squares, called "lights." The edges are sealed with copper foil tape. If you're not comfortable cutting the glass squares, have a glass and mirror shop do it for you.

MATERIALS

desiccant-dried primroses

unfinished wood jewelry box

1½" x 1½" (4 cm x 4 cm) glass tiles ("lights") cut from picture frame glass ¹⁄₁₆" (1 mm) thick*

¾" x ¾" (2 cm x 2 cm) vitreous glass tiles

copper foil tape

white sanded grout

craft acrylic paint in white and copper

clear-drying tile adhesive

V-notch trowel or flat-blade spreader

grout float

foam brush

small paintbrush

sponge

scissors

painter's low-tack masking tape

rubber gloves

spray glass cleaner

clean, soft cloths

paper towels

*Cut two glass lights for each flower tile desired

1 | Arrange the clear and colored tiles on the jewelry box cover to plan the design, allowing approximately ¼" (5 mm) between tiles for the grout. (With sanded grout, this larger spacing is recommended; use latex grout if smaller spaces are desired.) Remove the tiles, keeping them in order.

2 | Paint the jewelry box inside and out with two coats of white acrylic paint, letting dry after each coat. Load the small brush with copper paint. Paint a scroll accent across the front edge of the box in a loose and flowing stroke. Let dry.

3 | Clean the glass lights with glass cleaner, and dry thoroughly. Snip the stem from a flower and center the flower on one square of glass. Place another glass square on top, making sure all the petals lie flat. Hold the glass squares together firmly and run a length of copper foil tape along one edge, burnishing it with your finger to seal. Continue applying the tape all around, burnishing and sealing as you go. When you reach the starting point, overlap and trim the tape at the corner. Press any overhanging tape onto the front and back surfaces of the glass. Wipe the tape with a soft cloth to remove any fingerprints. Repeat for each tile desired.

4 | Apply tile adhesive to the jewelry box cover with a V-notch trowel or flat-blade spreader. Also brush adhesive on the back of each tile. Adhere the tiles to the jewelry box cover in the design mapped out in step 1. Let dry overnight.

5 | Protect the glass flower tiles and the sides of the box with low-tack masking tape. Mix some white sanded grout with water following the manufacturer's instructions. Put on the rubber gloves. Apply the grout to the tiled surface with a grout float, angling it to force the grout in between the tiles. Let the grout set 15 minutes. Wipe the tiles with a clean, damp sponge, and wait another 10 minutes. Remove the masking tape. Clean the tiles with a damp cloth, and then polish them with a dry cloth to remove any remaining haze. Let cure according to the grout manufacturer's recommendations.

BRANCHING OUT

Use any pressed flowers, either singly or in mini bouquets, to fill the glass tiles— you can even use single leaves. For a more random mosaic pattern, break the tiles into smaller pieces with tile nippers, as was done for the smaller yellow jewelry box. The mosaic doesn't have to be grouted; leaving the edges of the tiles exposed adds sculptural interest.

THE INSIDE DIRT

• Whether you buy primroses for this project or grow your own, avoid varieties with double blossoms. The multiple layers of petals will not press well.

• To best preserve the color, dry your primroses in silica gel. They will then naturally press out between the glass in this project.

BRANCHING OUT

It's difficult to varnish buttons without leaving behind sticky fingerprints or gumming up the holes. To make the job easier, build an inexpensive base from a large, thick piece of balsa wood and some toothpicks. Cut each toothpick in half and press the pointed ends into the balsa wood, side by side, using the button holes as a spacing guide. When you're ready to decoupage, simply push each button onto its toothpick holder—it will be held aloft, and you won't need to touch it while you work. As an added bonus, the toothpicks will keep the button holes clear of acrylic medium and varnish.

THE INSIDE DIRT

- Varnish can alter or fade the color of certain flowers, so it's always a good idea to test a few samples first.

- If fading does occur, you can use watercolors to reinforce or even change the flower color. Place the flower on a paper towel and lightly touch it up with water-thinned paint, brushing from the center outward. Let the paint dry completely before using the flower for crafting.

phlox button necklace

Pressed phlox flowers create a stylish statement on a button necklace. String a short necklace to wear as a choker, or a longer one for a more sophisticated look.

MATERIALS

pressed phlox flowers

13 to 18 large round buttons in peach, lavender, and green

black leather cord

2 small coil crimps

plated screw clasp

matte acrylic medium

satin water-based varnish

foam brushes

craft knife

jewelry pliers

1 | Using a foam brush, coat the surface of each button with matte acrylic medium. Place a pressed phlox flower on the damp surface, avoiding the button holes, if possible. Repeat for as many buttons as desired. Let dry completely.

2 | Apply one coat of satin water-based varnish to the surface of each button, and let dry. Use a sharp craft knife to carefully trim away any plant material covering the button holes.

3 | String flowered and plain buttons on the leather cord in a random sequence. Test-fit the strand periodically against your neck to determine the perfect length for your necklace.

4 | Fit a small coil crimp over each end of the cord, and pinch closed with pliers to secure. Separate the screw clasp into two pieces. Attach one piece to each end of the cord, using pliers to open and close the loops on the coil crimps.

polymer clay napkin rings

Bright and lively, these napkin rings are made by pressing fresh flowers into polymer clay.
The clay rings are then baked and glazed to keep the flowers' intense colors alive well past
the blooming season.

MATERIALS

assorted fresh flowers*

oven-hardening polymer clay

polymer clay glaze

rolling pin**

baking sheet**

craft knife

soft paintbrush

*Bidens, coreopsis, lobelia, and black-eyed Susan are shown

**Reserved for craft use

1 | Knead approximately two handfuls of polymer clay until it is smooth and easily workable. On a protected work surface, roll out the clay to a ¼" (5 mm) thickness.

2 | Use a craft knife to cut the clay into strips approximately 5" (13 cm) long x 1½" (4 cm) wide, or slightly narrower, if you prefer. Peel away and reserve the excess clay.

3 | Arrange fresh petals and flowers in a pleasing design on the middle of each clay strip. Press flowers firmly into the clay at the centers and around the edges to ensure that the botanicals stay embedded in the clay when it is manipulated.

4 | To shape the napkin ring, bring the ends of the strip together, flowers on the outside. Make sure the flowers remain pressed into the clay. Place each napkin ring flower side up on a cookie sheet. Repeat steps 1–4 to make additional rings, as desired.

5 | Follow the clay manufacturer's instructions to bake and cool the napkin rings. Check their progress at the earliest recommended time to prevent overbaking.

6 | Brush an even coat of polymer clay glaze on the front of each napkin ring, and let dry. Brush another coat of glaze on the bottom to complete the coverage, and let dry.

BRANCHING OUT

You can make beautiful flower tiles with polymer clay, or try jewelry such as pendants and earrings. Pierce a hole in the soft clay with a toothpick or nail to allow for chains and earring wires before oven-baking the finished design.

THE INSIDE DIRT

• Before making a complete set of napkin rings, bake a few sample pieces with your chosen flowers. That way, the exact baking time and temperature can be confirmed. Overbaking will cause the petals to curl inside their impressions.

• Use an oven thermometer while baking to make sure that the temperature is accurate.

• Testing will also let you discover which flowers, if any, do not work with this application. Some flowers change color dramatically when glaze is applied. Pink and red flowers, for instance, tend to brown.

BRANCHING OUT

Dried larkspur is a wonderful flower to use in interior floral arrangements. Its strong vertical appearance let's you experiment with height and dimension. You could change the levels of the different colors, or use them in smaller groups for a vibrant display.

THE INSIDE DIRT

• Larkspur air-dries beautifully. Simply hang it in small bunches in a warm, dark, dry location that has good air circulation.

• If you don't have access to a hydrangea bush, any sturdy leaf that has a firm vein structure can be substituted.

• If you are uncertain how much compound to use, make a few test prints on scrap wood first. A test print isn't absolutely necessary, however, as mistakes are easily sanded away when dry.

indoor window box

This colorful indoor window box can make it seem like summer all year long. The wooden box is relief-printed using a hydrangea leaf and joint compound, and the air-dried larkspur creates a thick hedge of color.

MATERIALS

air-dried larkspur*

fresh hydrangea leaf

unfinished wood box

dry floral foam

acrylic paint in off-white
and metallic peridot green

joint compound

spray matte acrylic varnish

scissors

foam brushes

soft, clean cloth

*We used three dried bunches each of dark pink
and purple larkspur

1 | Paint the unfinished box with one coat of off-white acrylic paint, brushing with the grain of the wood. Let dry.

2 | Coat the back of a freshly picked hydrangea leaf with a thin layer of joint compound. Center the leaf, coated side down, on the front outside wall of the box, and press with your fingers to transfer the compound. Remove the leaf carefully. Print two more leaves, one on each side of the first print. Let dry completely.

3 | Paint the entire box with another coat of off-white acrylic paint. Cover the leaves completely, but avoid filling in the relief details too heavily. Let dry.

4 | Mix one part metallic green paint with one part water. Using a soft, clean cloth, apply the green mixture to the box in broad strokes along the wood grain. Wipe away the excess paint, leaving behind a soft wash of color. Add more color to the leaf shapes only, allowing the paint to collect in the detailed areas. Let dry. Spray with matte acrylic varnish to finish.

5 | Pack the box tightly with dry floral foam, stopping 1" (3 cm) from the box rim. Sprinkle a light layer of dried larkspur leaves on the surface to prevent the foam from showing through the final arrangement. Starting at one end of the box, insert stems of dried pink larkspur into the foam, clipping them as needed to utilize the areas of fullest flowering. Pack the stems tightly next to each other and at the same height, for a solid, trimmed-hedge appearance. Change to purple larkspur at the middle, then finish with pink as shown. Add smaller stems to fill in around the perimeter where necessary for a full appearance.

woven lavender candle cuffs

Weave sweet-smelling air-dried lavender through wire-edged ribbon to make these decorative candle cuffs. The design is easily adapted to fit around candles of different sizes, from small glass votives to larger candle columns. Make certain that your votive is placed in a clear glass holder and that the lavender remains safely clear of the flame at all times.

MATERIALS

air-dried lavender

candle*

assorted wire-edged ribbons

thread to match ribbons

fine-gauge copper wire or green florist's wire

fabric glue

wire cutters

scissors

hand-sewing needle

low-tack painter's masking tape

*a votive candle in a clear glass holder
and a thick column candle are shown

1 | Divide the lavender into 16 to 24 bunches of three stems each. Trim the stems to a uniform length that is appropriate for the candle height, as shown in the photo. To secure each bunch, wind fine-gauge wire twice around the stems, and clip off the excess.

2 | Cut three to five 18" (46 cm) lengths of wired ribbon. Arrange the ribbons facedown on a flat surface, parallel to one another, leaving small spaces in between. Tape down the ribbons at one end with a piece of low-tack tape.

3 | Weave the stems of one lavender bunch through the ribbons, over and under. Repeat with a second bunch, alternating the weaving pattern. Adjust the wire bindings so that they fall directly on a ribbon, not in between or under, so that they will not show on the right side. Continue weaving in bunches of lavender, pushing them tightly together as you go, until you have enough to encircle the votive holder or candle. To check the length, secure the open ribbon ends with painter's tape and gently wrap the weaving around the glass votive or candle to see if the ends meet. Add or remove bunches as needed, leaving an even number on the cuff, and retape the end.

4 | Carefully wrap the weaving around the glass votive or candle, wire bindings on the inside, and bring the two taped ends together. Peel back the tape from the top ribbon on each side. Trim the ribbon ends so that they overlap about 1" (3 cm). Fold the top ribbon under for a neat finish, and join the overlap with a few drops of fabric glue. Reinforce the join by hand-tacking with needle and thread. Repeat to join the remaining ribbons. Retrim the bottom of the lavender stems if necessary, and double-check to make sure the wire wrappings are hidden.

BRANCHING OUT

Add other dried flowers, such as pink asters or orange strawflowers, to the ribbon area for a colorful accent. Simply glue them to the lavender weaving with a low-temperature glue gun. Or, use the ribbon and lavender weaving to cover a cylindrical lamp shade, accent a decorative birdhouse roof, or trim a picture frame.

THE INSIDE DIRT

• Harvest lavender at the base of its stem. It will dry well hanging in loose bunches.

• Lavender is covered in aromatic oil glands that emit a sweet, calming fragrance. It is also repellent to insects.

• In addition to the pale purple or "lavender" color for which the summer flowers on this evergreen perennial are best known, there are pink, blue, white, pale green, magenta, and deep purple blossoming varieties.

This chapter presents a variety of simple techniques for transferring botanical images onto everyday objects such as curtains, place mats, and pillows—giving them a stylish new identity. Whether you are looking to capture the intricate vein patterns in a leaf or the radiating petals of a flower, botanical imprints are a fabulous way to create memorable artistic images.

garden arts

As with all the crafts in this book, the projects are designed so that they are easy to make and open to variation, according to your tastes and available materials. Be sure to refer to "The Inside Dirt" for tips on finding supplies or making substitutions. Discover more project ideas that use the same techniques when you read "Branching Out." With a little ingenuity and creativity, you can make a variation on a project we show using materials you already have on hand. Or, you might use the techniques you learn here as a springboard to create something entirely unique.

BRANCHING OUT

Use the sun printing technique to illustrate the pages or cover of a garden journal. You can create a series of prints to frame, or you might make specialty designs for a decoupaged collage. Sun prints can also be used for other paper-crafted items, such as gift tags, greeting cards, and lamp shades.

THE INSIDE DIRT

• For those who do not have a garden plot, fresh herbs will grow just as happily in containers and pots on a terrace or stoop.

• Before combining herbs in pots, check to make sure they require the same degree of sunlight, soil depth, and moisture.

herb sun-print clock

Paper tile cyanoprints decorate a clock that's perfect for a gardener's kitchen. Simply place sprigs of fresh herbs—parsley, sage, rosemary, and thyme—on the pretreated paper and place in bright sunlight to make the intense blue exposures.

MATERIALS

fresh parsley, sage, rosemary, and thyme

nine 4" x 4" (10 cm x 10 cm) squares of sun-print paper

12" x 12" (30 cm x 30 cm) unfinished clock face

clock works and hands

acrylic paint in white, dark blue, and light blue

all-purpose paste-glue or PVA glue

clear acetate or transparency paper

photocopier access or black fine-point permanent marker

foam brush

small artist's paintbrush

fine sandpaper

baking sheet

scissors

ruler

numeral templates (see pages 116–117)

1. Paint the clock face with two coats of white acrylic paint, letting dry after each coat. Paint the molded edge light blue, and let dry. Use a small paintbrush to add a fine line of dark blue paint at the join between the flat surface and the molding. Let dry. Lightly sand the molded edge to distress the paint.

2. Photocopy the clock numerals on pages 116–117 onto clear acetate or transparency paper (or use a black fine-point permanent marker to trace and color the numerals on acetate by hand). Cut out each acetate template on the cutting line.

3. Read the manufacturer's instructions for the sun-print paper. Bring the fresh herbs, numeral templates, unopened package of sun print paper, and baking sheet outside on a sunny day. Working quickly, open the sun-print paper and place nine squares blue side up on a baking sheet. Position the four numeral templates on top of four sheets, making sure that the template edges extend past the edges of the sun print squares. Lay fresh herbs on eight squares, including parsley on the square with the number 12, sage on number 3, rosemary on number 6, and thyme on number 9. Leave the ninth square empty.

4. Immediately expose the paper and herbs to bright sunlight until the paper turns white, typically 1 to 5 minutes, depending on the conditions. Bring the baking sheet indoors, remove the herbs and numerals, and rinse the paper under running water for 1 minute. Lay flat to dry. As the paper squares dry, the areas that were exposed to the light will turn a rich blue, revealing photographic prints of the herbs.

5. When the paper is completely dry, trim each piece to 3¼" x 3¼" (8 cm x 8 cm). Referring to the photo, arrange the paper tiles on a flat surface as they will appear on the clock face. Lay the top left tile facedown on a protected work surface, brush a very thin coat of all-purpose paste or PVA glue on the back, and position the tile on the clock face. Press firmly to seal, and carefully remove any oozing glue. Glue on the remaining tiles in the same way, allowing an even space in between as a faux grout line. Let dry.

6. Attach the clock works and hands as directed by manufacturer.

pear-print place mats

Pear trees always produce more fruit than you can eat! Use the excess produce to print
these colorful, casual place mats, perfect for garden lunches or sunny breakfasts.

MATERIALS

purchased fabric place mats*

2 to 4 pears of different varieties

opaque fabric paint in brown, gold, green,
red, and yellow

iron

knife

fine paintbrush

watercolor palette

triangular cosmetic sponges

spray water bottle

paper towel

*Include extra place mats or fabric for test prints

1 | Slice a pear in half from top to bottom, directly through the stem, if possible. Place each half, cut side down, on a paper
towel for a few minutes to blot the juices.

2 | Pour a small amount of each of the opaque fabric paint colors onto the palette. Add a few drops of water to each color,
and mix well.

3 | Use lightly dampened cosmetic sponges to load the flat cut surface of one pear half with paint. Begin by sponging
yellow paint onto the entire surface. Add shading and detail with the gold, green, and red paints, using both the pear's
natural skin coloring and the photograph as a guide. Apply the paint fairly heavily, to facilitate blending and printing. Color
the edge and the stem with brown paint.

4 | Spray the painted surface lightly with water to blend the colors. Place the pear, painted side down, on the place mat.
Press evenly and firmly on the entire pear, including the stem, to transfer the paint to the fabric. Lift the pear carefully
to avoid smearing the print. You may want to do a few test prints on extra fabric before working on your final project.

5 | Repeat steps 3 and 4 to decorate all the place mats. If the stems don't print well, paint them in by hand using a fine
brush and brown paint. Let dry overnight. Heat-set the paint by ironing on the reverse side of the fabric according to
the paint manufacturer's instructions.

BRANCHING OUT

Instead of printing the pears in natural colors, try something bold. Go for solid bright colors in a grid pattern on primary colored place mats, à la Andy Warhol. Or, print pears on kitchen curtain valances or trim. Other varieties of produce would also make interesting prints: Try apples, mushrooms, or any fruit or vegetable that is fairly firm and has a distinctive shape.

THE INSIDE DIRT

- You don't have to have a pear tree growing in your yard for this project to be a success. Supermarket pears will work just fine. You'll find the greatest variety in the fall. The Bosc pear has a long, narrow taper to its neck. The Seckel pear is more rounded and petite.

- Use fruit that is firm, neither underripe nor overripe, and that has a well-developed core.

BRANCHING OUT

Create a strong and graphic design on the curtains by printing leaves in a repeating pattern or by using brightly colored fabric paint. Experiment with other fabric projects: plants with small leaves, such as fresh herbs, print more effectively onto proportionately smaller cloth items such as cotton napkins or a tea towel.

THE INSIDE DIRT

- Fresh leaves, not dried, work more effectively with this project. The vein structure is more prominent, making for a more detailed and interesting print.

- Each leaf can be reused about three to six times.

sheer leaf-print curtains

Beautiful, breezy, and fresh, these sophisticated white-on-white sheers are easy
to create with purchased curtain panels and a simple leaf printing technique.

MATERIALS

sheer white curtain panels

selection of fresh leaves with interesting
shapes and strong vein patterns*

opaque white fabric paint

triangular cosmetic sponges

straight pins

scrap kraft paper or newsprint cut
into squares slightly larger than the
selected leaves

brayer

tweezers

iron

*Featured: ferns and hibiscus leaves

1 Wash curtain panels according to manufacturer's directions to remove sizing. Press the curtains when dry, if necessary.

2 Place one panel on a firm but protected work surface (a large sheet of heavy corrugated cardboard is perfect since the curtain panel can be secured flat with straight pins directly to the cardboard). Place a piece of scrap paper underneath the fabric exactly where you wish to make one leaf print.

3 Place a leaf on a protected work surface. Dip a corner of a cosmetic sponge in the opaque white fabric paint. Dab the paint carefully on one side of the leaf, being careful to not overload the surface with paint. Note: results vary depending on which side of the leaf you use. Do at least one test print to see which side you prefer, and how much paint is appropriate for your design.

4 Carefully place the leaf painted side down on the curtain. You may find tweezers helpful when handling the painted leaves. Cover the leaf with another piece of scrap paper, and roll over the leaf two to three times with a brayer using firm but not heavy pressure to transfer the paint to the curtain. To avoid smears, don't let the leaf shift while rolling. You may also find that using your hands to press the leaf into the fabric is a successful alternative to rolling with a brayer.

5 Remove the protective scrap paper, and carefully lift the leaf from the fabric with tweezers. Let the paint set for a few minutes before proceeding. Repeat steps 2–5 as desired to cover the curtain panel with prints.

6 When curtain is completely dry, heat-set the paint by ironing on the reverse side of the fabric according to paint manufacturer's instructions.

radish tiles

Use real radishes and polymer clay to make dimensional tiles for your home.
A reusable mold is made from the clay first, and multiple tiles can be pressed from it.

MATERIALS

fresh radishes with their leaves

1.75 lbs (795 g) oven-hardening polymer clay

craft acrylic paint in moss green or salmon

burnt umber acrylic paint

acrylic glaze base

spray matte acrylic varnish

rolling pin*

baking sheet*

wooden pointed sculpting tool

craft knife

foam brush

soft, clean cloth

*Reserved for craft use

1. Knead half of the polymer clay until soft and workable. Roll it out on a baking sheet to make a slab ¾" (2 cm) thick and 6" x 6" (15 cm x 15 cm) square.

2. Select, wash, and dry three radishes and three well-formed leaves. Arrange the leaves on the clay, overlapping them as desired. Press the edges of the leaves with your fingers to firmly imprint them into the clay. Position the radishes on the clay, matching up the cut stem ends to the leaves, and press firmly to make an impression. Remove the radishes and leaves and discard them. Emphasize the leaf shapes by lightly outlining them with a pointed wooden sculpting tool. Bake the clay mold and let it cool, following the manufacturer's directions.

3. Knead half of the remaining polymer clay until soft and workable. Roll it out into a slab ½" (1 cm) thick and at least 5" x 5" (13 cm x 13 cm) square. Place the clay slab on the radish mold, covering the radishes but not completely covering the leaves. Press the soft clay into the mold, well into the radish forms. Peel the clay away from the mold, and place it, relief side up, on a baking sheet. Trim the edges with a craft knife to make a 4" x 4" (10 cm x 10 cm) square. Add an indented line border on the clean-cut edges with a wooden sculpting tool. Repeat with the remaining clay to make a second tile. Bake and cool the tiles according to the manufacturer's instructions.

4. Apply a solid coat of moss green or salmon acrylic paint to each tile. Let dry. Mix one part burnt umber paint with one part acrylic glaze base. Brush the glaze mixture on the tile, letting it fill the indentations. Wipe away the excess, leaving behind dark accents to highlight the shapes and impart an aged look. Let dry. Spray with matte acrylic varnish.

BRANCHING OUT

You can make similar tiles with other firm fruits and vegetables. Try peas, beans, baby carrots, and cherries. Create a grouped wall hanging with your tiles, or mount them on found barn wood for a custom frame. You can also trim the clay into other shapes such as circles, rectangles, and hearts. Adhere hanging hardware with strong glue.

THE INSIDE DIRT

• Radishes are one of the first crops that can be sown in spring, usually as soon as the soil is workable. They grow relatively fast, some varieties maturing in as little as a few weeks.

• If you are using purchased radishes for this project, make sure the greens are still attached and fresh.

BRANCHING OUT

Any fabric project would be enhanced by an image transfer. Try this technique on place mats and tablecloths, scarves and aprons, curtains and fabric lamp shades. It also works on wax candles.

THE INSIDE DIRT

• Choose light-colored flowers. They will appear as white with gray detailing when photocopied. If the flower image is too dark, the color of the fabric will not show through the transfer.

• For crisp images, select flowers with readily identifiable shapes and large details.

• Arrange the flowers as flat as possible on the copier bed.

pop art pillows

Let your cut flowers live on as bright and modern pillows. All you have to do is transfer their photocopied images to fabric. The simple technique utilizes wintergreen essential oil to affix black copier toner to the fabric. The transferred images will withstand hand washing as long as a natural fiber fabric, such as cotton, is used for the backing.

MATERIALS

fresh flowers*

100% cotton twill fabric, 1 yard (.9 meter) each bright pink, yellow, and green

thread to match fabric

fiberfill

transparent fabric paint (optional)

wintergreen essential oil

photocopier access

sewing machine

iron

rotary cutter, cutting guide, and mat

scissors

straight pins

craft knife

burnishing tool or spoon

cotton balls

*Sunflower, gerbera daisy, and white lily are shown

1. Wash and dry the fabric to remove any sizing, and iron flat.

2. Place a fresh flower facedown on the photocopier bed, but do not close the lid. Make a photocopy with black toner, enlarging the image as desired. (Be sure to look away from the light during copying.) Adjust the lightness/darkness setting to make the background dark and the flower light for maximum contrast. Try several different settings until you get the best exposure.

3. Use a craft knife and mat to cut out each flower. Cut a bit beyond the flower outline to create a dark, shadowy edge all around.

4. Place the fabric right side up on a firm, protected work surface. Place the flower cutout on the fabric, toner side down, and secure with straight pins. Dip a cotton ball in wintergreen essential oil, and rub it over a small section of the photocopy until it is saturated. Go over the damp area with a burnishing tool or the back of a spoon, rubbing firmly to transfer the toner to the fabric. You can lift a corner of the photocopy to check the progress, but be careful to reposition it exactly. Continue transferring the image in sections, removing the straight pins when necessary. Let dry.

5. To color the flower (if desired), use a foam brush to apply transparent fabric paint thinned with an equal amount of water. Test the results on scrap fabric first. If the paint is too watery, it will bleed beyond the transfer lines. If it is too thick, the black design will be hidden.

6. Fold the fabric in a double layer, image transfer on top, and place on the cutting mat. Use the rotary cutter and guide to cut the desired pillow shape from both layers, allowing an extra ⅝" (2 cm) all around for the seam allowance. We cut a 26" x 12" (66 cm x 30 cm) rectangle, a 16" x 16" (41 cm x 41 cm) square, and an equilateral triangle with a 24" (61 cm) edge. You could also use a commercial pattern to cut the pillow shape.

7. Place the two pillow pieces right sides together. Machine-stitch all around, making a ⅝" (2 cm) seam allowance; leave an opening on one side large enough for your hand to pass through. Clip the corners, turn right side out, and press the edges flat. Stitch ¼" (5 mm) from the edges all around, except at the opening. Stuff the pillow with fiberfill, placing it evenly throughout. Continue the stitching line to close the opening.

sun print hatboxes

Turn plain cotton fabric into a custom-designed botanical print. Simply treat the fabric with a special paint, lay the dried botanicals on top, and expose to the sunlight. Glue your newly printed fabrics around hatboxes to hold seed packets, crafting supplies, or photos of your garden.

MATERIALS

pressed botanicals*

3 papier-mâché circular boxes

white 100% cotton broadcloth

Pebeo Setacolor transparent fabric paints in Buttercup, Parma Violet, Moss Green, and Pernod Yellow

acrylic paint in white, yellow-gold, moss green, and purple

wide ribbon in coordinating colors

matte decoupage medium

spray adhesive

spray matte acrylic varnish

iron

scissors

straight pins

foam brushes

disposable cups for mixing paint

sheet of heavy-duty cardboard

large plastic garbage bag

*Hydrangea blossoms, Japanese maple leaves, and Queen Anne's lace are shown

1 | Machine-wash the cotton fabric to remove size. Dry and iron smooth. Rough-cut rectangles of fabric large enough to cover the sides of each of your chosen boxes, with some overlap on all sides.

2 | Mix the Buttercup and Parma Violet fabric paints with an equal amount of water, each in its own disposable cup. To obtain the green shade, mix equal parts of Moss Green and Pernod Yellow, and then mix in the water.

3 | Cover the heavy-duty cardboard with the large plastic garbage bag to make a protected, transportable work surface. Lay the fabric pieces on top. Spray or sponge the fabric with water to seal it to the work surface.

4 | Using foam brushes, apply the three diluted paints from step 2 to the three fabrics (one color per fabric) in smooth, broad strokes. Working quickly, place the pressed botanicals on the fabrics and press down firmly so they are secure. Bring the entire board into the sun. Wait 15 minutes, and then check the exposure by carefully lifting a corner of one botanical. When fully exposed (15 minutes to 1 hour), bring the entire board inside, remove the botanicals, and allow the fabric to finish air-drying. Iron the fabric for 2 to 3 minutes on the cotton setting to fix the paint.

5 | Apply one coat of white acrylic paint to each box. Let dry. Apply a coat of decoupage medium to the outside of one box with a foam brush. Carefully place the corresponding fabric piece on the wet medium, smoothing it carefully with your fingers. Overlap the ends, and leave some fabric overhanging at the top and bottom. Fold the excess at the bottom to the underside of the box, and glue down firmly with decoupage medium. Turn the excess at the top to the inside of the box, and glue in place. Glue a length of wide contrasting ribbon around the inside rim to conceal the raw fabric edges.

6 | Paint the box covers with acrylic paint to match the fabric, and let dry. Apply a wash of diluted white acrylic paint with a soft cloth, wipe off the excess, and let dry. Glue pressed botanicals to the cover with spray adhesive. Seal with a coat of spray matte acrylic varnish.

BRANCHING OUT

You can paint fabric in a wash of stripes and cloudy textures by brushing on one color first, leaving some areas white, and then filling the blank areas with another color. The diluted paints will bleed into each other, creating a soft yet vibrant effect. Use this fabric decoupage technique to make a journal cover, lamp shade, or picture frame. Or, use the finished fabric to create scarves, pillows, table linens, curtains, or patchwork quilts.

THE INSIDE DIRT

- Botanicals with distinct, recognizable shapes work best for this project.

- When pressing botanicals, make sure neither the petals nor the leaves overlap. Overlapping plant material will take away from the shape definition that is so effective with sun printing.

- Remember to press materials of like size and substance on the same sheet so that they dry at the same rate.

BRANCHING OUT

Try this decoupage technique on any wood surface. At most craft shops, you'll find a large selection of unfinished wood products, including frames, shelves, storage boxes, and cabinets. Instead of seed packets, use cutout words and images from flower and seed catalogs (arrange them in a collage) or color photocopies of botanical drawings from books.

THE INSIDE DIRT

• If a seed packet you want to use for this project still contains seeds, save them in a paper envelope (one type of seed per envelope). Be sure to label the type of seed and the date purchased on the paper envelope.

• Seal the paper envelopes in a plastic, zipper-locked bag along with a few grains of silica gel.

• Properly stored seeds can potentially keep for several years.

seed packet tea tray

Recycle colorful seed packages by gluing them onto a tea tray. This decoupage technique utilizes acrylic matte medium—a liquid easily found in craft and art supply stores—to glue and seal the paper to the wood surface.

MATERIALS

empty seed packets*

unfinished wood tea tray*

four basswood strips, each
24" x ¼" x ¼" (61 cm x 5 mm x 5 mm)

teak water-based stain

dark green acrylic paint

acrylic matte medium

satin water-based varnish

wood glue

craft knife, plus saw blade

straightedge

cutting mat

foam brushes

clean, soft cloth

*A 12" x 18" (30 cm x 46 cm) tray covered
with 18 packets is shown

1. Remove the hardware, if any, from the tea tray. Apply teak water-based stain to the surface with soft cloth, following the manufacturer's directions. Let dry.

2. Trim off all four edges of each seed packet, using a craft knife, straightedge, and cutting mat. Save the front panel of each packet.

3. Place one panel facedown on a protected work surface. Using a foam brush, apply acrylic matte medium to the back of the panel. Position the panel, glue side down, in one corner of the tray, and smooth in place. Repeat to adhere the remaining panels in a brickwork pattern, overlapping the edges slightly. Trim the last few panels as needed to fill out the edges. Apply a final thin layer of matte medium to the entire surface, and let dry.

4. Attach the saw blade to the craft knife. Cut the four basswood strips to size to line the inside edges of the tray floor, butting the ends at the corners. Paint the strips dark green, and let dry. Apply wood glue to two adjoining faces of each strip, and glue in place.

5. Apply three to four light coats of water-based varnish to the entire tray, letting dry after each coat. When completely dry, reattach the hardware.

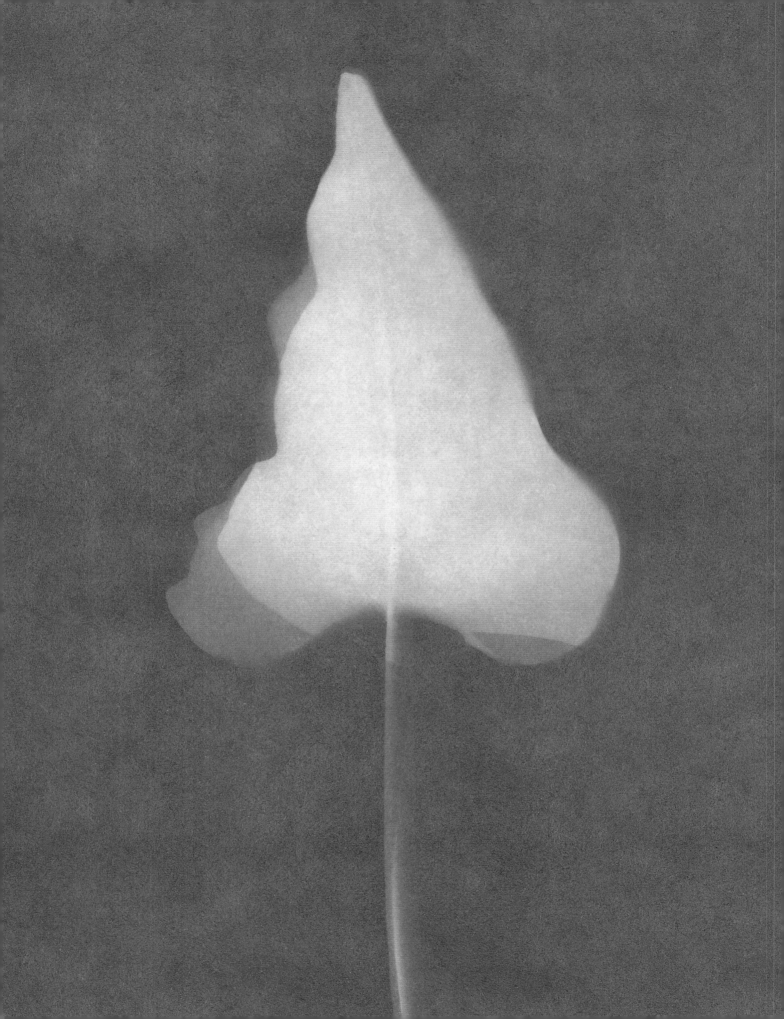

The garden is well known as a place that rejuvenates the body as well as the soul. This chapter explores various ways to pursue this end. Botanicals are used to make simple pro-jects intended for self-care or quiet moments of relaxation. From bath teas to sachets to soaps, this chapter in particular integrates aromatherapy with garden-inspired crafts. You'll find instructions for bath teas that take just minutes to make but can help take you miles away from your worries.

the garden spa

A bolster wrapped in candy-striped silk will certainly add an elegant touch to the head of a bed or end of a sofa. What is not so apparent is that the pillow is lined with crumpled, dried sage, the essential oils of which are said to inspire sweet dreams and rest. If anything, the crafts in this chapter are meant to remind us to stop and smell the roses—and anything else in the garden that prompts us to take a refreshing pause.

herbal-blend bath teas

In the dead of winter, the gentle aromas of homemade bath teas will bring your garden back to life. These bath tea pouches are made with inexpensive cheesecloth, so you needn't feel guilty about discarding the cloth after a few uses. As you prepare new pouches, you can reuse the ribbon and button tie. Hang the bag from your tub spout, or let it float freely in the bath water.

MATERIALS

tea blend of dried herbs and flowers*

cheesecloth

¼" (5 mm) sheer ribbon

vintage shank-style buttons

large-eyed needle

scissors

*See "Branching Out" for suggested blends

1. Fold the cheesecloth in a double layer. Cut through both layers, making an 8" (20 cm) square. Pour approximately ½ cup (.125 l) of the tea blend into the center of the cheesecloth square.

2. Cut a 32" (81 cm) length of sheer ribbon, trimming the ends diagonally to prevent fraying. Fold the ribbon in half, and tie an overhand knot at the middle of this shortened length. The large loop that is formed can be used to hang the bag on the tub spout.

3. Draw up and cinch all four corners of the cheesecloth with your fingers to create a pouch around the tea mix. To secure the pouch, place the knotted portion of the ribbon firmly against it and wrap the loose ends of the ribbon several times around in opposite directions. Tie once, without knotting. Thread the ribbon ends through the button shank, using the needle if necessary. Retrim the ribbon ends.

BRANCHING OUT

The following is a sampling of some of the herbs and flowers you might wish to use in homemade bath teas. They are categorized according to the effect their aromas tend to induce.

Soothing
lavender
chamomile
rose petals
lemon verbena
bergamot

Invigorating or refreshing
rosemary
jasmine
mint
rose geranium

Pleasing
lemon balm
pineapple sage
lemon verbena
mints
rosemary
scented geranium leaves
chamomile buds
sweet woodruff
lavender
bee balm

Muscle-relaxing
sage
rose
strawberry leaves
comfrey
rosemary
lavender

To add bright color accents
calendula
violets
nasturtium

THE INSIDE DIRT

- Screen-drying is the ideal way to pre-pare herbs and flowers for bath teas.

- If you are drying large quantities, use several screens and stack them on tin cans of equal size. This will save space but still allow ample air circulation.

- Store dried bath tea ingredients individ-ually or in blends in airtight containers.

- If the water from your tub spigot does not run very hot, make a concentrated bath brew. Heat a kettle of water on the stove until boiling. Place the bath tea pouch in a saucepan, pour in the boiling water, and let it steep a few minutes. Transfer the steaming concentrate to fresh bath water.

BRANCHING OUT

The essential oils of many herbs and flowers have distinct therapeutic effects, such as being relaxing or invigorating. See page 61 for a short list of herbs and their corresponding characteristics. For further information on this topic, refer to books on aromatherapy and herbal medicine.

THE INSIDE DIRT

• Use clear glycerin soaps if you want the botanical you are adding to be readily visible.

• Dried calendula, hibiscus, and rose hips retain their color well in these soaps. Most herbs, unfortunately, turn brownish in color.

• Always use dried botanicals when adding to soaps. Fresh botanicals can present bacterial problems.

real simple garden soaps

"Melt-and-pour" glycerin soaps let you make your own soaps without having to work with lye. You simply melt glycerin soap bases, pour the liquid into molds along with your favorite garden flower or herb, and wait a brief period for the soaps to harden. For these soaps, olive oil clear glycerin soap base and honey glycerin soap base were used in alternating layers with black-eyed Susans suspended in between.

MATERIALS

dried herbs, flower petals, or whole flowers

"melt-and-pour" glycerin soap

one essential oil, or more, of choice

soap molds or plastic containers

medium-sized saucepan

heatproof bowl and cover*

stainless steel spoon

*Choose a bowl that fits on the rim of the saucepan

1. Fill the saucepan about 2" (5 cm) deep with water, and bring to a gentle simmer. Set the heatproof bowl on top, making sure it does not touch the simmering water.

2. Add the soap to the heatproof bowl. Cover and let melt, stirring occasionally. Once fully melted, remove the bowl from the pan. Let cool slightly, about 2 minutes.

3. Stir in .5 to .7 ounces (14 to 20 g) of essential oil per 1 pound (457 g) of soap. If using petals or herbs that will be evenly distributed in the soap, stir them in along with the oil. Pour the liquid soap into the molds. Let sit until the soaps have firmed up.

4. To suspend a single flower or other botanical in the center of the soap, fill the mold only one-quarter to one-third full and let harden about 20 minutes. Then add the flower, followed by more soap mixture. (To make the soaps shown here, we added olive oil–based soap and honey-based soap in four alternating layers.) Let sit until the soaps have firmed up.

sage-lined bolster

The mellow aroma of common sage is known to have soothing, sleep-inducing effects—
perfect on a restless night or to encourage an afternoon nap. The sage in this bolster
is hidden from view, encased in a muslin liner, but its gentle aroma will nonetheless find
its way to your senses. When the essential oils in the sage dissipate, the liner can be
removed and replenished with freshly dried sage from a new season.

MATERIALS

dried and crumbled sage	sewing machine
striped fabric for pillow cover*	scissors
muslin or other natural cotton fabric*	hand-sewing needle
ribbon to match pillow cover fabric*	straight pins
thread to match pillow cover fabric	tape measure
bolster form (in desired size)	*Purchase sufficient fabric and ribbon for your size bolster

1. Measure the length and circumference of the bolster, and add 2" (5 cm) to each measurement. Cut two rectangles to these dimensions from muslin. Set the sewing machine to a short stitch length. Machine-stitch the rectangles together around three sides with a ⅝" (2 cm) seam allowance, leaving one of the "length" sides open. Clip the corners diagonally, turn right side out, and press. Loosely fill the muslin pocket with dried crumbled sage. Close the open edge by whipstitching by hand.

2. Bring the two "length" edges of the liner together, overlapping them slightly to form a tube, and whipstitch by hand. Pull the tube over the bolster. Adjust the sage filling so that it is evenly distributed around the bolster.

3. Remeasure the pillow length and circumference and add 1½" (4 cm) to each measurement. (With the added liner, the circumference should measure slightly larger than in step 1.) Referring to the diagram on page 118, cut one center panel rectangle to the new dimensions from striped fabric, stripes running parallel to the "circumference" edges. Cut two side panels with the stripes running the opposite way, making each panel at least twice as wide as the bolster diameter, or so that the ends can be folded and cinched.

4. Fold each side panel in half lengthwise, right side out, as indicated in the diagram. Press to set the crease. Pin the long raw edges to the center panel, right sides together. Machine-stitch, making a ⅝" (2 cm) seam allowance. Press the seam allowances toward the center panel. Fold the entire piece in half lengthwise, right sides together, and stitch the longer edges together to form a tube. Press the seam open. Turn right side out.

5. Gently insert the bolster into the striped tube covering until it is centered. Cinch the end panels with your fingers and tie with ribbon.

BRANCHING OUT

All shapes and sizes of pillows can be used for this project. The choice in fabric is virtually limitless. Do be sure, however, to use a natural-fiber fabric that breathes so that the aroma of the sage can be effectively diffused.

THE INSIDE DIRT

- Harvest sage foliage when it is perfectly mature, neither immature nor too old, to obtain peak levels of essential oils.

- Dry sage leaves on a screen or other surface that allows air to circulate, and be sure to place the screen in a dark, dry location.

- Sage is fully dry when it breaks crisply and crumbles readily.

BRANCHING OUT

Combine different colored fillings to change your decorating scheme quickly and easily. For a stronger visual effect, fill or top off one section with a single whole dried flower. Or, cover the petals and grains with a secure piece of glass, and turn the shadow box back into a wall-mounted display filled with home-spun items and colorful art.

THE INSIDE DIRT

• To make a simple, homemade potpourri, place dried petals, herbs, leaves, seeds, and spices in an airtight container. Place the container in a dark, dry, and relatively warm place. Store this way up to two months, turning the jar periodically to blend the contents.

• If a potpourri aroma fades or is faint from the start, revive it with a small piece of paper dabbed with essential oil. Add the paper to the jar and then reseal the jar.

petal potpourri tea-light holder

A purchased shadow box becomes an enchanting holder for deconstructed potpourri
and colorful grains, simply by adding dividers made of balsa wood. A faux zinc finish adds
an urban accent to the finished craft. Tea lights held in metal cups protect the potpourri
from the open flames, but even so, do not leave the burning candles unattended.

MATERIALS

assorted botanicals*

unfinished wood shadow box

balsa wood strips (the width should match
the box depth)

three tea lights

essential oil for the dried flower petals,
if desired

warm charcoal gray acrylic paint

silver metallic dry artist's pigment

clear paste furniture wax

clean, soft cloth

craft knife with fine saw blade

cutting mat

foam brush

*Air-dried rose petals, popcorn kernels, and soybeans
are shown

---

1 Cut three balsa wood strips, one the length of the inside box and two the width of the inside box. Mark each short piece
at the midpoint. Mark the longer piece in thirds. Cut a notch at each mark, stopping halfway through the strip. Test-fit
the balsa wood strips by interlocking the short pieces to the long piece at the notches. Trim the notches as needed until
the pieces fit together.

2 Paint the shadow box and balsa wood strips with two coats of warm charcoal gray acrylic paint, letting dry after each coat.

3 Tint some clear paste furniture wax by mixing in a small amount of silver metallic dry artist's pigment. Wipe the wax onto
the painted box and balsa wood with a clean, soft cloth. Remove any excess wax, and let dry. Buff with a clean cloth
to a soft sheen.

4 Assemble the painted balsa wood strips to make the inside dividers. Place the assembly into the shadow box. Fill the
sections with selected dried petals and grains, and add tea lights where desired.

no-sew organza sachets

These sachets just might be too pretty to hide away in a drawer or a closet. Made of metallic organza, frayed silk dupioni trim, and button or beaded accents, they pay a nod to modern elegance as well as a little well-deserved indulgence. All of the pieces are joined with fusing tape, making it easy to make up multiples for gifts. The fusing tape also helps prevent the sheer organza from fraying at the seams.

MATERIALS

dried flower petals, herbs, or potpourri

metallic organza fabric

matching metallic silk dupioni fabric

buttons, beads, or other small accents

thread

⅝"-wide (2 cm) paper-backed fusing tape

iron

hand-sewing needle

1 | Cut an 8½" x 15" (22 cm x 38 cm) rectangle from the sheer organza fabric. Fold it in half crosswise to make a pocket, and press to set the crease. Fuse the side edges together, following the fusing tape manufacturer's instructions and placing the tape ¼" (5 mm) in from the edges. After fusing, trim the sides even with the outer tape edge to make an 8" x 7½" (20 cm x 19 cm) pocket.

2 | Cut a 9½" x 4" (24 cm x 10 cm) rectangle from the metallic silk dupioni, so the nub runs parallel to the longer edges. Referring to the diagram on page 119, fold the rectangle in half, wrong side in, and press to set the crease. Open up the rectangle. Fold and press each short edge ¾" (2 cm) to the wrong side for the flaps. Pull out a few threads along both long edges to create a fringed effect.

3 | Lay the silk dupioni wrong side up on the ironing surface. Following the diagram, cut and fuse tapes 1, 2, and 3 in position on section A. Let cool. Peel off the paper backing. Position the open end of the organza pocket over section A, aligning the raw edges on the fold. Fuse in place, and let cool. Next, cut and fuse tapes 4 and 5 to the flaps, and let cool. Peel off the paper backing, fold in the flaps, and fuse in place.

4 | Place a modest amount of dried petals, herbs, or potpourri in the sheer pocket. Fuse tape 6 in position on section B, overlapping the flaps, and let cool. Peel off the paper backing. Fold section B down onto section A, enclosing the top of the sheer pocket, and fuse in place. (Be sure to push sachet contents to the pocket bottom, out of the way of the iron.) Embellish by sewing on accent buttons or beads.

BRANCHING OUT

To make a drawstring-style sachet for hanging, follow the same technique to make the sheer pocket. Then fold in the top edge by about 1¼" (3 cm) and fuse in place to form a casing. Thread a ribbon through the casing and cinch closed to create a purse effect. Embellish with beads at the ribbon ends or attach a beaded fringe along the sachet base.

THE INSIDE DIRT

• To fill sachets, use dried petals from your favorite fragrant flower, an air-dried insect-repellent herb, such as lavender, or a potpourri of flowers and herbs.

• Regardless of the filler chosen, you may want to boost the fragrance with a few drops of an essential oil. Choose an oil-bearing scent of an ingredient in your potpourri mix or a scent that complements your dried flowers or herbs.

BRANCHING OUT

If you prefer to make a larger votive, use proportionately larger flowers. This is also a great way to capture the bright colors of autumn leaves.

THE INSIDE DIRT

• Choose petite yet bold flowers with very little overlapping of petals. The flowers must be pressed well to avoid air pockets in the design.

• If using leaves, do not let them dry to the point of brittleness, or they will crackle when they are molded around the votive.

• Fibrous rice paper tears more easily if you crease it first. Run your fingernail or the handle of a spoon along the fold line to set the crease.

petite botanical votive set

On each of these small, narrow votives, a single pressed flower is muted by a layer of translucent rice paper. The edges of the paper are torn and stop short of the votive rim and base for a soft, organic look. Aside from the time it takes for the glue to dry, this project requires just fifteen minutes of hands-on attention.

MATERIALS

pressed flowers*

3 glass votives with candles

translucent rice paper

decoupage glue

foam brush

steel cork-backed ruler

spray glass cleaner

paper towels

*Coreopsis is shown

1. Lay the paper on a flat surface. Place the steel ruler on top, hold it down firmly, and tear the paper by drawing it up along the ruler edge. Use this method to tear a rectangle for each votive, large enough to wrap around once and overlap by at least ¼" (5 mm). Make the height of the rectangle slightly less than the votive, to show a bit of the glass rim and base.

2. Remove the candles, and clean and dry the glass votives. Using the foam brush, apply a thin, even coat of decoupage glue to the glass at the spot where the flower will be placed. Carefully position the flower on the glass, making sure there are no wrinkles or air bubbles in the petals. Let dry in place.

3. Gently apply a thin, even coat of glue to the glass votive where the paper will be applied. Starting at the back, position the edge of the paper on the glass, then slowly wrap the paper around, smoothing out any wrinkles and air pockets as you go. Apply another thin, even coat of glue over the paper. Let dry overnight.

flower waters in etched bottles

Lightly fragranced waters in etched bottles add a personal accent to your home spa decor. Etching is much simpler than you might think, but do be sure to wear protective gloves and eyewear when using the highly caustic etching cream.

MATERIALS

rose or lavender water (see page 73)

glass bottles with cork stoppers

etching cream

craft knife

self-adhesive shelf lining paper

carbon transfer paper and pen

rubbing alcohol

cotton swab

foam brush

rubber gloves

protective eyewear

etching patterns (page 120)

1   Remove the stoppers from the bottles, wash the bottles, and let air-dry completely.

2   Cut a 3" x 3" (8 cm x 8 cm) square of self-adhesive shelf lining paper. Transfer one of the etching patterns from page 120 to the center of the paper with transfer paper and a pen.

3   Remove the backing from the shelf paper. Press the paper, adhesive side down, on the glass bottle, so that the design is well positioned on the bottle's surface. Cut out the design carefully with a craft knife. Peel off the cutout sections of the design to be etched.

4   Burnish the remaining pieces of the design firmly onto the glass with your fingernail. Clean the exposed glass area with a cotton swab dipped in rubbing alcohol, and let dry.

5   Wearing protective clothing as recommended by the manufacturer, use a foam brush to apply a thick, even coat of etching cream to the exposed areas of the design. Keep the cream from touching any glass on the perimeter of the shelf paper. Let sit as recommended, usually from 5 to 12 minutes. Rinse the cream completely from the bottle, remove the shelf paper mask, and let the bottle dry to reveal the etched design.

6   Repeat steps 2–5 for each bottle. Fill the finished bottles with flower waters and replace the cork stoppers.

THE INSIDE DIRT

- If rose or lavender is not your fragrance of choice, there remains a wide choice of other flowers and essential oils that you can use alone or in combination to make floral or herb-scented waters.

- As with perfume, consider the characteristics of a flower, herb, or essential oil. Seek balance, combining an aroma that is stimulating with one that is calming and then punctuating the two with a strong middle note, something decidedly in between.

RECIPES

For rose water:

- 1 cup (.25 liter) packed fresh deep red rose petals (approximately 6 large garden roses)
- 2 cups (.5 liter) boiling distilled water
- ¼ cup (.06 liter) vodka
- few drops of rose essential oil (optional)

For lavender water:

- ½ cup (.125 liter) dried lavender
- 1 cup (.25 liter) boiling distilled water
- ¼ cup (.06 liter) vodka
- few drops of lavender essential oil (optional)

Place the lavender or rose petals in a clean, sterilized glass container. Pour the boiling distilled water over the botanicals. Add the vodka, seal, and let steep for one week. Strain the waters, add essential oil if desired, and funnel into decorative bottles.

Just as a garden is about vitality and vibrance, it is also about stillness and peace. The projects in this chapter reflect the Zen-like aspect of natural objects. From a mirror framed with sand and garden pebbles to an Asian-influenced money plant lamp shade, each project assumes a simple, understated approach.

from the zen garden

Of all the chapters, this one works with the greatest variety of materials and perhaps the most eccentric. The delicate dry, outer skins of garlic and onions are used to make tiny bowls. A Zen centerpiece is assembled from river stones, Spanish moss, and strawflowers. They are the type of projects that inspire the imagination as well as instruct the mind. Consider what materials you have readily available and how you might adapt and modify a project in order to make use of them. That way, instead of waiting to craft later, you can begin in the Zen now.

BRANCHING OUT

This mosaic technique is a perfect decoration for memento and jewelry boxes or clock faces. You can also use it to accent backsplashes, table tops, headboards, or even a chair rail in a beach house.

pebbles and sand mirror

Even the pesky pebbles from your garden can be put to good use in this Zen garden–inspired frame. A mixture of tile adhesive and craft sand makes a textured grout that will hold your found pebbles securely in place.

MATERIALS

collection of pebbles

unfinished wood frame with a flat surface molding

dyed desert craft sand in tan, dark brown, and natural

burnt umber acrylic paint

hanging hardware

clear-drying mosaic tile adhesive

clear furniture paste wax

putty knife

foam brush

measuring cup

clean, soft cloth

large disposable container and stirrer

1. Paint the frame with the burnt umber acrylic paint, and let dry. Add hanging hardware to the back of the frame, if desired.

2. For a large frame (cut the following recipe in half for a small frame), combine ½ cup (.125 liter) natural craft sand with ¼ cup (.06 liter) each dark brown and tan sand. Place the combined sands, 1 cup (.25 liter) clear-drying tile adhesive, and a large spoonful of water in a disposable container, and mix well. Add more sand, adhesive, or water as necessary to make a smooth, thick, spreadable mixture. The texture and consistency should resemble creamy peanut butter.

3. Prop the frame, right side up and level, on some old jars or cans over a protected work surface. Spread the sand mixture evenly over the front and sides of the frame with a putty knife. The mixture will self-level and maintain a smooth surface on the top, but you may need to even out and reapply the sides manually a few times.

4. When the frame is completely covered, let the sand mixture set for 10 minutes. Scrape any drips off the bottom edges as they occur.

5. Set the pebbles firmly into the sand mixture. Let dry completely. Dip a clean cloth in furniture wax and lightly wipe the pebbles to accentuate their colors and provide a protective finish.

garlic skin bowls

In a technique resembling papier-mâché, garlic skins are layered and overlapped to make delicate bowls, perfect for storing potpourri, small beads, or specialty salts, such as those shown here. The skins were curled back at their tips to create the blossomlike appearance. The process is meditative, and no two bowls look alike.

MATERIALS

several bulbs of garlic*

PVA glue (neutral pH adhesive)

spray varnish

craft knife

small, sharp scissors

small soft paintbrush

disposable plastic container

aluminum foil

*Red onion skin bowls also shown here

1. Use a craft knife to cut through the dry, delicate outer skin of the garlic bulb, starting at the base and working toward the tip. If possible, run the blade between the two cloves of garlic that lie underneath. Make three or four cuts around the head so that you can peel off the outer skin in large pieces. Carefully slice them free from the base and set them aside. The remainder of the garlic can be used for cooking.

2. Crumple and wad the foil into a small ball the size of a finished bowl. For garlic skin bowls, 1½" to 2" (4 cm to 5 cm) in diameter is ideal. Flatten one side of the ball slightly, so that it will sit on the work surface without rolling.

3. In a disposable plastic container, dilute some glue with three times as much water. Sit the foil ball on a protected work surface. Place one piece of garlic skin over the top of the ball, letting it drape down one side. Lightly brush the end near the top with diluted glue. Place another layer of skin on top of the ball, draping it toward the opposite side. Repeat to cover the entire ball, brushing glue wherever the papery skins overlap.

4. When the skins have dried enough to hold their place, remove the foil ball. Curl back the tips of the skins to create a blossom effect, if desired. Let dry completely. Apply spray varnish. If the bowl will be used to hold salt or any kind of food, be sure to use a food-safe varnish.

BRANCHING OUT

Try adhering small pressed flowers to the outside or inside of garlic or onion skin bowls. Or, use flower petals instead of the skins to make the bowls. Dry the petals partially, not all the way. If they are fully dried, they will be too crisp to mold around the foil ball. Leaves are another possibility.

THE INSIDE DIRT

• If you purchase garlic or onions to make this project, look for clean, thick, unblemished skins. Use the dry outer layers only. The waxy interior layers, particularly of onions, do not take to the glue and are apt to decompose.

• If you are growing your own garlic, try varieties with red or purple-tinted skin for this project. Elephant varieties have cloves that are large and distinct, which makes the outer skins somewhat easier to release.

• Collect garlic and onion skins over time, as you do your routine cooking. Store the collected skins in a shoe box or other protective container until you are ready to use them.

BRANCHING OUT

Texture is the key to filling this centerpiece. You can also use landscaping stones, cedar, or other ornamental garden fills. Instead of using a shadow box, fill separate matching elements, such as four soy sauce dishes, four rice bowls, or four decorative ashtrays. Protected tea lights could be added, but make sure to supervise their burning.

THE INSIDE DIRT

- Strawflowers and other "everlasting" flowers can be found year-round in the dried flower section of most craft stores.

- If you grow your own strawflowers, harvest them when the buds just begin to bloom. They will open further as they dry.

- The stems on strawflowers weaken as they dry. If you wish to maintain the stems, support the flowers on a mesh screen, letting the stems dangle underneath so that they aren't crushed.

zen-inspired centerpiece

Turn a shadow box into an Asian-inspired centerpiece by filling it with items of distinctive texture. Polished stones, gravel, bamboo, and moss combine for a "four seasons" theme, and dried strawflowers float on the surface, like water lilies on a calm pond.

MATERIALS

finished wood shadow box

polished river stones

marble river gravel

bamboo

Spanish moss

air-dried strawflowers

dry floral foam

craft knife with fine saw blade

cutting mat

ruler

1. Cut the floral foam to fill the shadow box, stopping 1" (3 cm) from the rim. Mark the foam surface into four equal quadrants. Cut away the foam in one quadrant to half its thickness. Reserve this quadrant for the Spanish moss, which needs more space to fill in evenly.

2. Fill one quadrant with polished river stones, confining them to their section by selecting larger stones to edge the rectangle. Fill the gaps with smaller stones so that the floral foam doesn't show through. Fill an adjoining quadrant with marble river gravel, keeping it within the rectangle's borders.

3. Measure one side of the third quadrant. Cut lengths of bamboo to this measurement, using a craft saw and cutting mat. Cut as many as are needed to fill the quadrant, mixing thick and thin stalks for variety, if desired.

4. Fill the remaining, deeper quadrant with Spanish moss until it reaches the same level as the stones and bamboo. Place dried strawflowers in a random pattern on the centerpiece's surface.

pea pod vase

There's nothing sweeter than peas picked fresh from the garden! But do save
one pod to imprint this air-dried, paint-glazed terra-cotta vase.

MATERIALS

pea stalk with pea pod and leaves

Mexican terra-cotta clay

waterproof sealer

craft acrylic paint in white and soft green

premixed acrylic painting glaze
in metallic gold

spray matte acrylic varnish

rolling pin*

craft knife

scissors

soft paintbrushes

foam brush

clean, soft cloth

disposable container with cover

templates (see page 121)

*Reserved for craft use

1. Photocopy the patterns (page 121) onto plain paper, and cut out them out to make the templates.

2. Place a small handful of clay in a disposable container. Cover with water, seal the container, and let sit overnight. This makes "slip," a jellylike substance that will be used later to adhere the clay slabs together.

3. On a protected work surface, roll out a slab of clay to a ¼" (5 mm) thickness. Place the template pieces on the clay surface, and cut out the shapes with a craft knife. Remove the excess clay.

4. Place a pea pod with a small amount of stem on an angle near the top of the rectangular slab. Add groups of leaves, vein side down, and tendrils, creating a pleasing pattern around the pod. Be sure to place the pod and stems at an angle to the sides of the slab, or they will crack open when the vase is assembled.

5. Roll the rolling pin over the pea leaves and pod, pressing them into the clay. Don't roll too heavily over the pod. Carefully press each leaf even more firmly into the clay with your fingers.

6. Score a row of X's along the two shorter side edges of the slab. Use a soft brush to apply slip to these edges. With the pea greens still embedded in the clay, shape the slab into a cylinder, butting the short edges. Score a ring of X's on the sides of the circular base and the bottom inside edge of the cylinder. Brush the scored edges with slip, and join the base to the cylinder. Carefully remove the pea greens. Wipe the joined edges with a soft brush and more slip until well sealed and smooth. Let dry for 48 hours.

7. Apply water-based sealer inside and out with a foam brush, and let dry. Dip a clean cloth in white acrylic paint. Working in horizontal strokes, wipe a coat of paint across the vase. Make sure that the pea and leaf impressions fill with paint to accent them. Wipe away the excess paint to leave a light wash. Let dry.

8. With a small soft brush, apply green acrylic paint to the leaves and pea pod, and again wipe away the excess to leave a soft color-washed surface. Let dry.

9. Using a clean cloth, wipe a light coat of premixed metallic gold decorative painter's glaze across the surface of the vase. Wipe away any excess paint as desired and let dry. Spray with one coat of matte finish acrylic varnish.

BRANCHING OUT

Make a few small clay pieces with pea imprints on them for experimentation with different finishes—try a dark brown wash to accent the imprints, or any other combination of acrylic paints, rub-on wax finishes, or paint glazes. You can also make flower or fall leaf imprints in the clay.

THE INSIDE DIRT

- You don't need a garden plot to make this project—the peas used to imprint this vase were grown in containers on a deck.

- This project can be ideal for peas that have passed their peak of sweetness. Peas with toughened pods that are more pronounced in form will make well-defined imprints.

BRANCHING OUT

Mulberry paper provides the perfect absorbent yet lightweight paper for screened projects. Watercolor paper is a good choice for flower-pounding projects that require a heavier paper. Create special greeting cards and frameable art from your pounded flower experiments. Or, fill a journal, writing the name of each flower next to the pounded print for future reference. You can also pound flowers onto fabric treated with a mordant.

THE INSIDE DIRT

• Of the many flowers tested for this project, cosmos, pansies, scavola, and rose vinca were superior. Pink impatiens created a subtle but pleasant dye transfer. Note that white flowers do not transfer, not even onto dark-colored paper.

• If a flower's pistil is fleshy, it will get mashed in the transfer and ruin the paper. In such cases, pluck the petals individually and transfer in a reassembled form.

pounded flower night-light shade

Flower pounding provides immediate gratification—the beauty of the natural dyes
from freshly picked flowers is intense and evocative. This shoji screen–inspired shade
can be hung on a small nail in front of a wall outlet to give a conventional night-light
a new look. Leave the sides of the shade open for easy access to the night-light's
on-off switch, or line the sides with more pounded leaf prints.

MATERIALS

assorted fresh flowers*

mulberry paper

¼" x ¼" (5 mm x 5 mm) basswood, four
6" (15 cm) strips

¼" x ¹⁄₁₆" (5 mm x 1 mm) basswood, two
4½" (11 cm) strips, two 4" (10 cm) strips,
and four 2" (5 cm) strips

black acrylic paint

white craft glue

PVA glue (neutral pH adhesive)

hammer

foam brush

paper towel

*Recommended are cosmos, rose vinca, scavola,
and pink cascading petunias

1. Place a sheet of mulberry paper on top of four sheets of paper towel. Lay your chosen freshly picked flowers facedown on the mulberry paper, and cover with an additional paper towel. Pound the surface with a hammer until you see the natural flower dyes seep through the top paper towel. You can check your progress by lifting just the edge of a petal. Make sure that you've pounded all the surface area of the flower for an even transfer to the mulberry paper. Peel off the flower, and let the transfer dry. Not all flowers will transfer well; be prepared to experiment with many varieties, and watch them over time. Some will seem to work but then fade or discolor over the course of a few days.

2. Paint the twelve basswood strips with black acrylic paint. Let dry. To assemble the front frame, use white glue to join two 4½" (11 cm) and two 6" (15 cm) strips together, allowing a ¼" (5 mm) overhang at all corners. For the back frame, glue two 4" (10 cm) and two 6" (15 cm) strips together, overhanging at the top and bottom edges only. Let dry.

3. Join the front and back frames at the longer edges by gluing on four 2" (5 cm) strips, two on each side, to make a three-dimensional box. Hold together by hand for a few minutes, or until the glue sets. Support, if necessary, and let dry completely.

4. Trim one pounded flower print into a rectangle that will fit inside the front frame. Fold the long edges of the paper rectangle to lay flat against the vertical basswood strips. Brush PVA glue on the four inside edges of the front frame. Place the paper rectangle against the glued surface, and run your finger lightly along the edges to seal the paper firmly to the basswood frame. Let dry. Glue flower print panels in the side frames if desired.

money plant and
bamboo lamp shade

Delicately shingled money plant seed pods add fragile elegance to a purchased lamp shade.
Bamboo stalks define the faces of the shade and add their unique texture to the finished project.

MATERIALS

money plant seed pods

bamboo

white four-sided lamp shade

low-temperature glue gun

glue sticks

fine-blade craft saw

scissors

1 | Cut the money plant seed pods from their stalks with scissors.

2 | Place the lamp shade on the lamp base to suspend it above your work surface. Work on one plane surface of the shade at a time. Using the glue gun, apply a bead of glue horizontally across the bottom edge. Quickly and firmly press money plant seed pods in a row along the glue line, overlapping them slightly and overhanging the bottom edge of the shade.

3 | Apply a second horizontal bead of glue just above the first row of seed pods. Place a second row of seed pods, overlapping the first row in a shingle pattern. Continue gluing on seed pods in rows until one face of the shade is covered. Repeat for the remaining sides.

4 | Using a fine-blade craft saw, cut four lengths of bamboo to conceal each corner edge of the shade. Glue in place. In the same way, cut four shorter lengths to trim the top edges, and glue in place.

BRANCHING OUT

You can cover a cone-shaped lamp shade, too—just skip the top edging of bamboo and extend the side bamboo accents past the top and bottom of the shade to mimic an umbrella frame. The delicate money plant "shingles" are not appropriate for projects that will receive a lot of handling. Save them for decorative vases, night-lights, wall sconces, and paneled screens.

THE INSIDE DIRT

- Money plant, also known as honesty, is a natural for air-drying. Just hang it by the stem.

- You can also use silica gel to dry the money plant's seed pods.

The following pages contain an array of simple ideas and quick ways to bring the garden into your home. Each includes brief crafting tips, how-to instructions, and/or variation suggestions. And each is meant to underscore how

gallery of quick decorating ideas

garden-grown items and found objects can be used to make simple, low-budget gifts and decorative accents. Let the ideas you find here trigger brainstorms of your own. Like any true gardener or crafter, you are always ready to be inspired. Be resourceful, expect the unexpected, and enjoy the process.

chili pepper kitchen accents

Here's a hot tip: Add spice to your kitchen decor with dried chili peppers! String them on lightweight wire along with painted glass beads and dried peli nuts (both easily found in bead stores) to make a stylish window swag. Or, hot-glue a few peppers to the top of a wooden recipe box. For a rustic finish, color the box with water-based cranberry stain, sand the edges, and top with a light wash of white pickling gel. Drying peppers is as easy as drying flowers. Harvest them when ripe, then string them in bunches through their stems using a needle and thread. Hang them in a well-ventilated location until they are dry. Note: Use caution when handling chili peppers to avoid skin and eye irritaion.

sunflower curtain tieback

This curtain is cinched with a ribbon made from thinly peeled bark and studded with a single bright, wispy sunflower. The large flower was dried in two stages. First, it was set facedown in silica gel. Once the petals were dry, it was turned over and and the thick calyx and stem were sunk into the gel. To prevent the delicate petals from breaking off, a clear-drying glue was applied to the base of each one. The flower stem was inserted through a small hole in the ribbon and glued in place.

garden spigot hooks

Here's a whimsical way to hang your garden tools and sun hat. Create a series of hooks with purchased or vintage garden spigots and wooden rosettes—unfinished ornamental squares with a circular design already cut onto the surface. First, finish the wood rosettes as desired. We chose bright oil-based stains that are heavily pigmented yet transparent (see Craft Resources on page 122). Then, mount a spigot to the center of each rosette with two brass screws. Look for spigots with a notched flange for easy assembly.

burlap floor cloth with vegetable-dyed trim

Dyeing is a subtle but time-honored way to make botanicals a component of your handcrafted projects. Here, a burlap floor cloth is trimmed with a beet-dyed fringe. Some garden plants are classics for making natural dyes: yarrow, goldenrod, marigold, blueberries, tomatoes (the skins only), beets, and cranberries. But nearly every plant will yield some color, whether it's from the leaves, fruit, petals, bark, or roots. Often, a mordant is used with natural dyes to help set the color. The most common and least toxic mordant is aluminum potassium sulfate, also known as alum or alum salt. Used sometimes in pickling, alum may be purchased in most grocery stores.

garden boutonniere

Half the fun of growing your own fruits and vegetables is preserving the bounty in the form of jams, chutneys, sauces, and relishes to enjoy and share throughout the year. Instead of sticking the same predictable label on your canning jars, use natural resources from your garden to decorate the packaging. Here, elements from a berry plant were used as an identifying "boutonniere" for a jar of strawberry jam. What looks like a flower on this simple boutonniere is actually the leafy top of a strawberry. The top was hollowed out and dried in silica gel. An immature berry, plucked from the strawberry plant once it stopped bearing fruit, was dried and inserted through the top's hollow center. For a jar of pickles, you could use a dill blossom. But don't feel obligated to coordinate the boutonniere to the jar's contents. A dried flower would look just as attractive.

pressed petal
votive candles

If you have just a few pressed blooms left over from a project,

try this quick technique for decorating purchased votive candles.

Simply brush the side of a candle with candle and soap medium,

a fast-drying liquid that seals wax finishes. While the medium

is still wet, press the botanicals onto the candle surface. Brush

a second coat of the medium over the flowers to seal them in place,

and let dry. Clever arrangements of clover leaves, phlox, primroses,

bidens, and hydrangea petals can add pattern and color to plain

candles. Do a test candle with each botanical first, as some flowers

lose their pigmentation after exposure to the candle medium. And,

as always, carefully monitor votive candles while they are lit.

kitchen herb bouquet vase

When your garden is bursting with fresh herbs, bring daily clippings into the kitchen so they are readily at hand as you cook. For a simple, poetic touch, place them in cylindrical vases, shown here wrapped in a rice paper with springlike, spearmint-colored striping. The paper is lashed in place with hemp twine, making it easy to change papers with the seasons or on a whim. For an accent, insert a twig from a wild grapevine through each knot. You might also try a dried flower.

espresso cup centerpiece

Brighten up your table setting with tiny espresso cups filled with mini bouquets of dried flowers or dried

petals, such as our bunches of two air-dried strawflower varieties, desiccant-dried species rose petals,

and screen-dried species roses. When the party's over, let guests take their cups home as favors. If you're

feeling extra creative, put a "green thumb" on each purchased cup using a thumbprint stamp and green

oven-firing craft enamel paint made especially for use on already glazed ceramics. Simply paint the stamp's

printing surface with the enamel, blot lightly on a paper towel, and press onto the surface of the cup,

carefully rolling the stamp once from side to side for even coverage. Mistakes can easily be wiped from

the cups with a damp cloth before baking. Follow the paint manufacturer's directions for surface prepara-

tion and oven firing. Tip: If your bouquets need a bit more stability to stand straight, fill the cup partway

with dried beans to provide a base for the stems.

layered petal centerpiece

Make a room bloom with unexpected color as well as graphic style when you layer petals in a deconstructed potpourri. Combine different shapes of clear glassware as we have here, and fill them with complementary colors for a group centerpiece. Or, fill a single large glass vase or canning jar with layer upon layer of petals. We've combined lavender with lona (African daisies), red garden rose petals with statice, and pink cluster roses, heads still intact, with their leaves. All of the flowers were air-dried.

dahlia and moss picture frame

Revitalize a flea market find with dried flowers, sheet moss, and a glue gun. First, paint an unfin-

ished or unattractive frame with a coat of olive green acrylic paint, and let dry. Apply sheet moss

to the frame's surface with a low-temperature glue gun. Finally, glue desiccant-dried yellow dahlias

randomly on the surface. Your final product will make a sunny, carefree addition to your home.

Try other combinations of dried botanicals, too, with or without the moss underlayer.

flower art

Use antique wallpaper to create romantic, vintage settings for your favorite blooms. If you don't have sheets of old wallpaper, improvise with color photocopies of new vinyl wall coverings (paint and wallpaper stores often have sample books of discontinued wallpapers that they will give you for free) or sheets of paper gift wrap. Cut a piece of basswood to the size of the frame backing, and glue the wallpaper (or facsimile) to it using acrylic matte medium or wallpaper paste. When the glue is dry, sand the paper lightly to distress the finish, and age it by applying an uneven wash of strong cold tea. When the piece is completely dry, attach your chosen botanicals to the paper surface with a low-temperature glue gun or tacky floral glue. Desiccant-dried dahlia and air-dried cornflowers and bleeding heart are shown here.

french country hanging pots

Add Mediterranean flair to your patio or entryway by stringing together small terra-cotta pots that have been colorwashed in a bright French country palette. Begin by painting the pots with yellow and blue acrylic paint, brushing smoothly in one direction and then wiping off some of the wet color with a paper towel to reveal streaks of the underlying terra-cotta. Next, run string or twine through the drainage hole of each pot, knotting it at the point where each pot will sit. Tie a loop at the top for hanging, fill the pots with bunches of dried flowers, and voilà! Shown here are air-dried asters and statice and desiccant-dried marigold heads.

templates
and diagrams

Several of the projects in this book require templates or diagrams. To make a template, trace or photocopy the pattern printed in this section and then cut it out, as directed in the project instructions. Use the diagrams to guide you in cutting and placement decisions as you make a project.

Photocopy at 100%

12

3

6

9

sage-lined bolster (shown on pages 64-65)

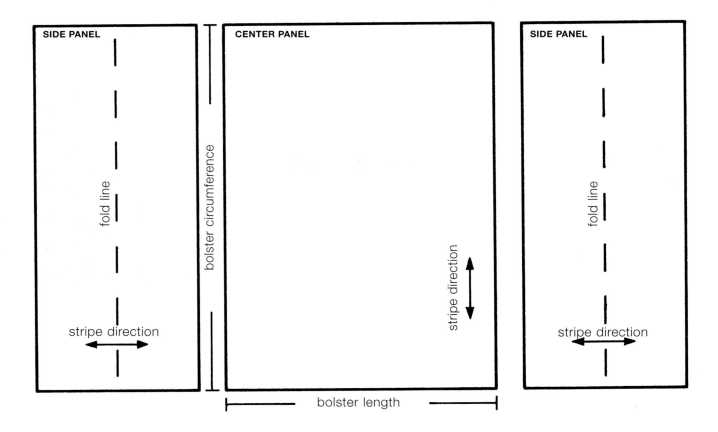

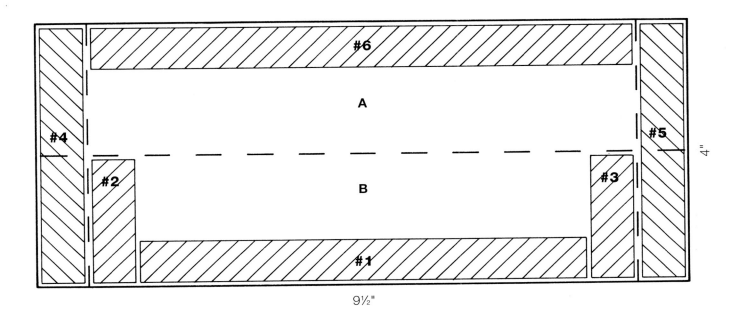

9½"

4"

⅝" (2 cm) paper-backed fusing tape

flower waters in etched bottles

(shown on pages 72-73)

Photocopy at 100%

pea pod vase (shown on pages 82-83)

Photocopy at 100%

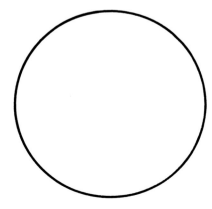

craft resources

The following mail-order resources offer a variety of traditional as well as unique craft supplies, including some of the harder-to-find materials used in this book.

Britex Fabrics
146 Geary Street
San Francisco, CA 94108
415-392-2910
www.britexfabrics.com
info@britexfabrics.com

Four floors' worth of fabric, buttons, ribbons, trim, and notions; fabric swatches available by mail for a small fee.

Delta Ceramcoat
www.deltacrafts.com

Candle and soap painting medium, acrylic paints, and sealers.

From Nature With Love
890 Garrison Avenue
Bronx, NY 10474
1-888-376-6695
www.fromnaturewithlove.com

Melt-and-pour soap bases, wide selection of essential oils, soap molds, and other soap-making supplies.

Gane Brothers & Lane, Inc.
1-800-323-0586

*Distributors of Yes! Glue, a thick,
transparent paste-glue with very good
lay-flat properties for paper.*

HobbyCraft
(stores nationwide)
Head Office
Bournemouth
01202 596100
United Kingdom

Basic craft supplies.

John Lewis
(stores nationwide)
Head Office
Oxford Street
London W1A 1EX
020 7269 7711
United Kingdom

Basic craft supplies.

Mosaic Mercantile
P.O. Box 78206
San Francisco, CA 94107
877-9-MOSAIC (toll-free)
415-282-5413 (fax)
877-708-2111 (toll-free fax)
www.mosaicmercantile.com

*Mosaic tile, grouts, primers,
and adhesives.*

Pebeo of America, Inc.
P.O. Box 717
555 Route 78, Airport Road
Swanton, Vermont 05488
819-829-5012
819-821-4151 (fax)
www.pebeo.com

*Setacolor Soleil Sunprinting Paint,
20 water-based, brilliant colors;
completely nontoxic, mixable,
and permanent once ironed.*

Rubber Stamps of America
160 Emerald St
Keene, NH 03431
1-800-553-5031
Fax: 1-603-352-0265
www.stampusa.com

Rubber thumbprint stamp

Walnut Hollow
1409 State Road 23
Dodgeville, WI 53533-2112
1-800-950-5101

*Unfinished wood crafts available
at leading craft departments throughout
the country; call for the nearest location.*

Woodburst Color Company
woodburst.com

*Brightly colored transparent pigmented
oil-based stain.*

garden resources

The Flower Depot
P.O. Box 654
Tonganoxie, KS 66086
1-877-780-2099
www.flowerdepotstore.com
www.thewreathdepot.com

*Dried and preserved botanicals,
wreaths, swags, and craft supplies.*

Loose Ends LLC
P.O. Box 20310
Keizer, OR 97307
503-390-2348
503-390-4724 (fax)
www.looseends.com

*Papers, dried botanicals, home
and garden accessories.*

Michaels
1-800-642-4235
michaels.com

*Silica gel desiccant, wide selection
of craft supplies.*

Nature's Pressed
P.O. Box 212
Orem, UT 84059
801-225-1169
800-850-2499
801-225-1760 (fax)
www.naturespressed.com

*Flower presses; pressed flowers,
ferns, foliage, herbs, and leaves.*

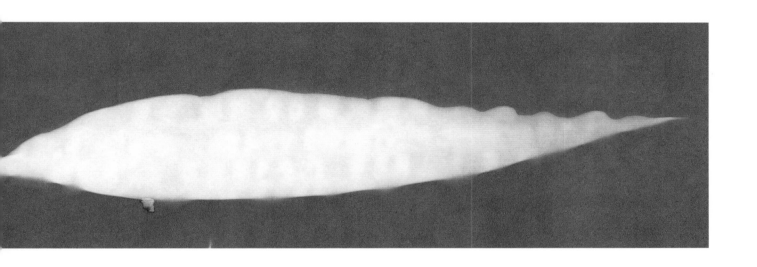

about the authors

Influenced by her master gardener father and decorator mother, **Sandra Salamony** is especially gifted at combining botanicals with nontraditional crafting techniques. Most recently the author of *Hand Lettering for Crafts*, she has also collaborated with Mary Ann Hall on *The Crafter's Project Book*, both published by Rockport Publishers. Her craft designs have appeared in many books and magazines.

Maryellen Driscoll, a tireless writer, crafter, gardener, and cook, lives on a small working farm at the foot of the Adirondack Mountains. A former editor at *Cook's Illustrated*, she is author of *The Paper Shade Book* and has contributed to several national magazines and major newspapers.

acknowledgments

This book would have remained just the sprout of an idea without the help of many others. We'd like to thank all of the talented people at Rockport Publishers for helping *A Gardener's Craft Companion* to grow, especially Mary Ann Hall, who had the foresight to bring two authors with individual strengths yet similar ideas together on this book. Candie Frankel also deserves a big round of applause for organizing the production of this book and remaining steadfast and calm throughout all the deadline pressure. To Claire MacMaster, many thanks for the use of your home and garden for the beautiful photography, and kudos to the talented Silke Braun for leading the art direction of the book.

Many manufacturers contributed their products, which were invaluable to ensure that we explored the full range of crafting options. So, special thanks to The Flower Depot, Loose Ends, Mosaic Mercantile, Nature's Pressed, Pebeo Paints, and Walnut Hollow! And, thanks to Bonny's Garden Center, especially Sal, who gave us "first pick" of all the fresh flowers for testing. Finally, warm appreciation to our friends and coworkers, who gave us flowers from their gardens and ideas from their experience, and who patiently listened when projects didn't turn out quite as planned.

On a personal note, Sandra would like to thank her sister, Gina Brown, for being a close friend throughout the years and providing inspiration through good, clean, sisterly competition (and for helping complete all those childhood garden chores!). And thanks to Katy (from Maryellen) for offering a fresh perspective on colors, combinations, and approach—and for trekking through the thistle to find the field of flowers.